Ideas and Ideologies
General Editor:
Eugene Kamenka

Human Rights

**Edited by Eugene Kamenka
and Alice Erh-Soon Tay**

St. Martin's Press
New York

© Edward Arnold (Publishers) Ltd. 1978

All rights reserved. For information, write:
St. Martin's Press, Inc., 175 Fifth Avenue, New York, N.Y. 10010
Printed in Great Britain
Library of Congress Catalog Card Number 78-4469
ISBN 0-312-39960-X
First published in the United States of America in 1978

Library of Congress Cataloging in Publication Data

Main entry under title:
Human rights.
  Bibliography: p. 133.
  Includes index.
  1. Civil rights—Addresses, essays, lectures. I. Kamenka,
Eugene. II. Tay, Alice Erh-Soon.
JC571.H768   323.4   78-4469

Contents

Introduction

The conception of human rights is of central importance in the development of the modern world. Like all such ideas, it is very much theory-laden, implying a general view of man and society, of individuality, politics and the ends of government. Like all such ideas, it is profoundly historical, expressing the aspirations and seeking to remedy the ills of particular places and times. It is thus an idea with a history, an idea that changes in both content and social function.

In this volume, the second in the series 'Ideas and Ideologies', the development of the idea of human rights, the internal complexities of that idea and its place in the world today are discussed by lawyers, philosophers, a historian of ideas, a political scientist and a sociologist—all of them thinkers of international repute with a substantial interest in the subject. The papers have arisen out of a course on human rights taught to senior law students taking jurisprudence in the University of Sydney, from a series of public lectures organized by me for the Australian National University and out of a human rights symposium and a special working session on human rights held as part of the World Congress of the International Association for Philosophy of Law and Social Philosophy in Sydney and Canberra in August 1977. The contributors to this volume all took part in some of these activities, several of them in all. The editors served as honorary secretary and president, respectively, of the Congress; the papers by Mr Benn, Dr Kleinig and Professor Wellman are those they presented as convenors-rapporteurs of the Congress working session on human rights to summarize and guide the discussions. This volume thus owes a special debt to the Congress that brought several hundred legal philosophers and social theorists from more than thirty countries together and to the donors who made that Congress possible—including the Utah Foundation, the Committee for Postgraduate Studies in the Department of Law in the University of Sydney, the Government of the Commonwealth of Australia, the

Government of the State of New South Wales, UNESCO, the Australian National University, the Australian Academy of the Humanities, the Faculty of Law in the University of Western Australia, the University of New South Wales, the New South Wales Bar Association, the University of Newcastle, the Academy of the Social Sciences in Australia, the Australia-Japan Foundation and the Faculty of Law in the University of Queensland, as well as a number of others.

Mrs Vibeke Wetselaar, Mrs D. J. Mitchell and Miss Margaret O'Neill have been put to infinite pains, both by the World Congress and the preparation of this volume; we are very grateful to them. We also owe much to Mrs E. Y. Short, who checked the manuscripts and proofs and prepared the index.

Canberra, September 1977   Eugene Kamenka

I

The anatomy of an idea

Eugene Kamenka

I

The eighteenth century, in Europe and America, drew to its close as the century that had clearly and unequivocally proclaimed the inalienable and imprescriptible rights of man. The proclamations were not, to begin with, the creatures of Gallic enthusiasm, of a revolutionary category of reason run riot in human affairs. They were the product of sober English philosophies, English puritanism and nonconformism, 'respectable' English resistance to absolutism and concern for freedom and toleration. They drew above all on the philosophy of John Locke and the traditions of the Glorious Revolution of 1688, with its Act of Settlement and compromise, non-individual, Bill of Rights, but with its muted undertones of the great trial of Charles I in 1649. That trial may have had the most dubious standing legally; the king for once may have confronted his accusers with dignity and much logic on his side. But the trial, as the regicides said later, was not 'a thing done in a corner', not an assassination or a summary execution. It was a bungled, illegal, but breathtakingly daring trial of a king *as king*, for failing in his duties to his subjects, for committing *treason* against a new implicit sovereign, the people. Its implications were world-shaking and they came to fruition a hundred and thirty years later, in the declaration dated 12 June 1776. That was

A Declaration of Rights

Made by the Representatives of the good People of Virginia, assembled in full and free Convention, which rights do pertain to them and their posterity as the basis and foundation of government.

1 That all men are by nature equally free and independent, and have certain inherent rights, of which, when they enter into a state of society, they cannot by any compact deprive or divest their posterity; namely, the

enjoyment of life and liberty, with the means of acquiring and possessing property, and pursuing and obtaining happiness and safety.

II   That all power is vested in, and consequently derived from, the people; that magistrates are their trustees and servants, and at all times amenable to them.

III   That government is, or ought to be, instituted for the common benefit, protection, and security of the people, nation or community; of all the various modes and forms of government, that is best which is capable of producing the greatest degree of happiness and safety, and is most effectually secured against the danger of maladministration; and that, when a government shall be found inadequate or contrary to these purposes, a majority of the community hath an indubitable, unalienable, and indefeasible right to reform, alter or abolish it, in such manner as shall be judged most conducive to the public weal.

The remainder of the declaration, articles IV–XVI, indeed, is concerned neither with revolutionary transformation nor with the metaphysical elevation of man, but with insisting on the separation of the legislative, executive and judicial functions, the election and accountability of 'magistrates' whose office derives from personal worth and on provision for proper legal procedures and governance by law.

The next declaration, 'The unanimous Declaration of the thirteen united States of America', made on 4 July 1776 echoed these sentiments in words known to almost every schoolchild:

We hold these truths to be self-evident, that all men are created equal, that they are endowed by their Creator with certain unalienable Rights, that among these are Life, Liberty and the pursuit of Happiness. That to secure these rights, Governments are instituted among Men, deriving their just powers from the consent of the governed, That whenever any Form of Government becomes destructive of these ends, it is the Right of the People to alter or to abolish it, and to institute new Government, laying its foundation on such principles and organizing its powers in such form, as to them shall seem most likely to effect their Safety and Happiness.

Fifteen years later, after the great revolution in France, the French National Assembly promulgated, as a document prefixed to the constitution, its Declaration of the Rights of Man and of Citizens—a declaration firmly rooted, in language and in sentiment, in the American declarations and the political and philosophical tradition that shaped them. In the translation popularized almost immediately by Thomas Paine's *Rights of Man*, the French declaration of 1789 read:

The representatives of the people of France, formed into a National Assembly, considering that ignorance, neglect, or contempt of human rights, are the sole causes of public misfortunes and corruptions of Government, have resolved to set forth in a solemn declaration, these natural, imprescriptible, and inalienable rights: that this declaration being constantly present to the minds of the members of the body social, they may be for ever kept attentive to their rights and their duties; that the acts of the legislative and executive powers of government, being capable of being every moment compared with the end of political institutions, may be more respected; and also, that the future claims of the citizens, being directed by simple and incontestible principles, may always tend to the maintenance of the Constitution, and the general happiness.

For these reasons, the National Assembly doth recognize and declare, in the presence of the Supreme Being, and with the hope of his blessing and favour, the following *sacred* rights of men and of citizens:

I   Men are born, and always continue, free and equal in respect of their rights. Civil distinctions, therefore, can be founded only on public utility.

II   The end of all political associations is the preservation of the natural and imprescriptible rights of man; and these rights are liberty, property, security, and resistance of oppression.

III   The nation is essentially the source of all sovereignty; nor can any individual, or any body of men, be entitled to any authority which is not expressly derived from it.

IV   Political liberty consists in the power of doing whatever does not injure another. The exercise of the natural rights of every man, has no other limits than those which are necessary to secure to every *other* man the free exercise of the same rights; and these limits are determinable only by the law.

V   The law ought to prohibit only actions hurtful to society. What is not prohibited by the law, should not be hindered; nor should any one be compelled to that which the law does not require.

VI   The law is an expression of the will of the community. All citizens have a right to concur, either personally, or by their representatives, in its formation. It should be the same to all, whether it protects or punishes; and all being equal in its sight, are equally eligible to all honours, places, and employments, according to their different abilities, without any other distinction than that created by their virtues and talents.

VII   No man should be accused, arrested, or held in confinement, except in cases determined by the law, and according to the forms which it has prescribed. All who promote, solicit, execute, or cause to be executed, arbitrary orders, ought to be punished, and every citizen called upon, or apprehended by virtue of the law, ought immediately to obey, and renders himself culpable by resistance.

VIII   The law ought to impose no other penalties but such as are absolutely and evidently necessary; and no one ought to be punished, but in virtue of a law promulgated before the offence, and legally applied.

IX   Every man being presumed innocent till he has been convicted, whenever his detention becomes indispensable, all rigour to him, more than is necessary to secure his person, ought to be provided against by the law.

X   No man ought to be molested on account of his opinions, not even on account of his *religious* opinions, provided his avowal of them does not disturb the public order established by the law.

XI   The unrestrained communication of thoughts and opinions being one of the most precious rights of man, every citizen may speak, write, and publish freely, provided he is responsible for the abuse of this liberty, in cases determined by the law.

XII   A public force being necessary to give security to the rights of men and of citizens, that force is instituted for the benefit of the community and not for the particular benefit of the persons to whom it is intrusted.

XIII   A common contribution being necessary for the support of the public force, and for defraying the other expenses of government, it ought to be divided equally among the members of the community, according to their abilities.

XIV   Every citizen has a right, either by himself or his representative, to a free voice in determining the necessity of public contributions, the appropriation of them, and their account, mode of assessment, and duration.

XV   Every community has had a right[1] to demand of all its agents an account of their conduct.

XVI   Every community in which a separation of powers and a security of rights is not provided for wants a constitution.

XVII   The right to property being inviolable and sacred, no one ought to be deprived of it, except in cases of evident public necessity, legally ascertained, and on condition of a previous just indemnity.

By 24 June 1793, in a new declaration, the French had proclaimed that the goal of society is the common happiness and that government is established to guarantee to man the enjoyment of his natural and imprescriptible rights, which are those of equality, liberty, security and property. In yet another declaration, prefixed to the constitution of 5 Fructidor of the Year III (22 August 1795), these rights were defined in articles 2–5:

2   Liberty consists in the ability to do that which does not harm the rights of others.

3   Equality consists in that the law is the same for all, whether it protects or punishes.

---

[1] The French text simply says 'has a right'.

Equality does not admit any distinction of birth, any inheritance of power.

4 Security results from the cooperation of all in assuring the rights of each.

5 Property is the right to enjoy and to dispose of one's goods, one's revenues, the fruits of one's labour and industry.

In these declarations lies the whole philosophy of liberal democracy in whose name most of the political struggles of the nineteenth century and many of the twentieth were to be fought. It had, and has, its critics. The guarantee of political rights and political equality contained in this constitution, the young Marx commented scathingly, was accompanied by and promoted the guarantee of the economic rights of property, and the social inequality which they necessarily produced. Behind the republic of the market lay the despotism of the factory; behind political equality lay social inequality.

The eighteenth century invented the idea of happiness, in which the concept of natural rights as political rights was deeply grounded. It also invented the idea of revolution, an idea that was to dominate much of Europe in the nineteenth century and all of the world in the twentieth. The slogan 'Liberty, Equality, Fraternity' could be read politically, but it could also be read socially, as calling for an economic, social and cultural reconstruction of society that went far beyond the political claims of the American revolutionists. The history of the doctrine of natural rights from the eighteenth century onwards, with the shift to a doctrine of human rights and of economic, social and cultural rights, can be seen as the story of the increasing concretization of rights, of an overcoming of their abstractness. But it is also the story of new and different concerns, of battles with different enemies, of demands that have quite new implications. The demand for rights in the seventeenth and eighteenth centuries was a demand *against* the existing state and authorities, against despotism, arbitrariness and the political disfranchisement of those who held different opinions. The demand for rights in the nineteenth and twentieth centuries becomes increasingly a *claim upon* the state, a demand that it provide and guarantee the means for achieving the individual's happiness and well-being, his welfare. These two different conceptions of rights, as we shall see, like the opposed conceptions of 'freedom from' and 'freedom to', stand in constant danger of fundamental conflict with each other—a conflict that dominates our contemporary world.

II

The belief in human rights as a great moral value, a UNESCO symposium characteristically insists, is not a specifically Western or Judaeo-

Christian contribution to the world. It is to be found in all the great moral documents of mankind, and in all its aspirations since primitive times. If the concept of human rights is to have any specific meaning, is to be seen as implying a view of man and society, this is untrue. The concept of human rights is a historical product which evolves in Europe, out of foundations in Christianity, Stoicism and Roman law with its *ius gentium*, but which gains force and direction only with the contractual and pluralist nature of European feudalism, church struggles and the rise of Protestantism and of cities. It sees society as an association of individuals, as founded—logically or historically—on a contract between them, and it elevates the individual human person and his freedom and happiness to be the goal and end of all human association. In the vast majority of human societies, in time and space, until very recently such a view of human society would have been hotly contested; indeed, most cultures and languages would not have had the words in which to express it plausibly. Of course, all human societies have had a concept of suffering and most of them have had a concept of human worth, of justice, of fair dealing, of meeting one's obligations. But the society of the great seventeenth- and eighteenth-century social contract theorists, the society of the right-and-duty-bearing individual standing in external 'contractual' association with other right-and-duty-bearing individuals, the society which the great German sociologist, Ferdinand Tönnies, called the *Gesellschaft*, is a modern, European phenomenon. The Greeks, like the Chinese, saw man in a familial, social and cosmic setting; and their concern was not with rights but with duties, and with balance, harmony, *moira*, *dikē* and *ius*, a balance that transcended the individual, that made society part of a great cosmic pattern and that rested on a network of obligations, not just to individuals but to forces and institutions, human and divine, that shaped and transcended such individuals. Men in pre-modern societies lived in a *Gemeinschaft* that saw man as part of a social organism, a structured community based on a common religious tradition, a hierarchy of power, a network of mutual obligations that made and shaped men, rather than served them. Even in Roman law as the Romans and their immediate successors knew it, there was a concept of right, and certainly of duties—but no concept of rights.

The story of the growing belief in natural or human rights as the eighteenth century saw them is the story of the rise of individualism in the theory and practice of society. Marxists link this with the growth of commodity-production, the development of cities and the merchant-burgher and the increasing importance of the bourgeoisie. Max Weber, in an account not so fundamentally different from Marx's, throws the emphasis on the emergence of a Calvinist Protestant ethic that made capitalism possible. Both accounts have their severe and effective critics. Many factors, related and unrelated, endogenous and contingent, have gone into the making of modern society and the ideologies of modern man. Those that have shaped and made possible the doctrine of the rights of man are those that help to undermine traditional society, the attitudes and values of the *Gemeinschaft*, the belief in cosmic forces and social hierarchies, powers and institutions that precede and transcend the individual man—even if the belief in such rights could emerge as confidently as it did only by anchoring itself, in the first place, in religious conviction and the authority of divine creation and revelation, understood in a new spirit.

Mr Minogue argues in the next chapter of this volume that the doctrine of natural rights is in no way a deduction from the doctrine of natural law but, on the contrary, involves a rejection of its ordered hierarchies and transcendent plan. Men saying something profoundly new frequently latch on to an old terminology to conceal the revolutionary nature of their views. I believe he is right, but I also believe that the Christian-Stoic readiness to counterpose a *ius naturale* and a *ius gentium* to the positive law of a particular state and to judge the latter in the light of the former, like the counterposing of Christ to Caesar, was a crucial precondition to the notion that man's natural rights could be counterposed to the rights actually granted him by the state in which he lived and used to reject that state and its arrangements. The idea of revolution and the idea of human rights as inalienable and imprescriptible require that a transcendent moral order should be set against the mundane municipal order in which we live and the insistence that that confrontation takes place in *this* world. The great monotheistic religions—Judaism, Christianity and to some extent Islam—drove to this confrontation; the great religions and social ethics of the East—Hinduism, Buddhism and Confucianism—did not. At the same time, despite many countervailing trends, Christianity and Roman private law, for different reasons, elevated the individual as the centre of moral and legal life. Christianity was about man, the man who had broken free of the *patria potestas*, whose individual moral freedom and responsibility were symbolized by the Man who hung on the Cross. 'Jurisprudence', says Title I of Book I of the *Institutes* of Justinian, 'is the knowledge of things divine and human, the science of the just and the unjust;' but it adds that the study of law consists of two branches, the law public and the law private, and that the law private relates to the advantage of the individual citizen, while the law public relates to the advantage of the Roman state. The Roman state was soon dead and gone and the law that related to it had nothing to say to later generations in different circumstances. The reception and modification of Roman private law, mingled with Christian precepts and canon law, and increasingly purged of historically specific Roman attitudes and practices and enriched by a new concern with sovereignty and relations between states, had a pervasive influence on the legal and political attitudes and practices of Western Europeans. The traditions and procedures of common law and the seventeenth-century reinterpretation of its history and spirit, the myth of the ancient constitution and the Norman yoke, and the possibility created by the earlier new humanism of looking back to the concept of citizenship and of politics as the 'science of freedom' created, in a different spirit, by the Greeks—all these, together with Roman private law, laid further indispensible foundations for the doctrine of the rights of the individual and provided much of their content and the form in which they were expressed. The Great Code of Punishments of the Ch'ing dynasty was as complex and sophisticated an administrative document as any European *lex* or *leges* up to even the nineteenth century; but it was a code of punishments, addressed to officials and not to the citizens, providing administrative measures, imposing strict obligations while encouraging *ad hoc* justice and sub-legal settlement. It laid no foundation for a doctrine of fixed and defined individual rights and powers; it stood with Persia, and not with Greece, in making all men servile, in creating what Herodotus saw as universal public slavery.

Of even greater importance as immediate preconditions for the development of a doctrine of human rights are, without question, the struggles of church, kings and barons in European feudalism, the consequent multiplicity of power centres and the importance of legal-contractual relations between them, the 'liberties' granted in feudalism, especially to cities, and the possibility of maintaining such a grant, charter or deed against the grantor himself even if he be king. It is this reality which is reflected in Magna Carta and that made it possible for the opponents of the later European absolutism to claim that the past was on their side. Just as important was the struggle, within the Christian church, against papal absolutism and religious hierarchy—the Conciliar movement, the popular interpretation of Wycliffe's doctrines, the rise of protestantism as the affirmation of the individual conscience against church precepts, the wars in the Low Countries, the formation of the new civil religion. And of course, from John Ball to the Levellers, there was the constant possibility of appealing to earlier and simpler times, in both church and state, when, allegedly, there was no papal or episcopal authority, when kings were elected, when men were rude but free and comparatively equal:

> When Adam delv'd and Eve span
> Who was then the gentleman?

Nevertheless, the seventeenth-century Englishmen who proclaimed their rights against kings and established church, and the social contract theorists, from Hobbes to Locke and Rousseau, were doing something startlingly new, at least at the level of respectable rather than underground ideology. They were claiming 'liberty' and not 'liberties', and beginning to assert general and not specific rights. They were radically reinterpreting and recasting the language of politics and of social and religious theory. They were proclaiming that the constitution of society was not divinely ordained, that society was not a system of separate historic estates, each with their specific and limited interests, and that the affair of state, the *chose publique*, was not the special and particular prerogative of the king and his governors. They were converting men from subjects into citizens. The point of the social contract was to establish this new conception of public power and of the relationship between the individual and society. The individual suddenly, and on a general scale for the first time, became the point of it all, standing as citizen in direct and not indirect relationship to public affairs and government, insisting that it existed for *his* advantage and that alone. The theory of the social contract could argue, as Hobbes did, that, once men had surrendered their powers, for their own security, to a sovereign, they had virtually no rights left but a very attenuated right to rebel if their continued existence was threatened. Even so, the theory established the principle that the basis and end of government was the security, the happiness, the rights of the individual. It is with that recasting of political language and ultimately of political reality that the modern individualist, democratic age begins. And while the roots of this development were nourished especially strongly by religious conceptions and religious conflicts and martyrdoms, the eighteenth century with its doctrine of the rights of man represents both a new and more thorough-going aspiration toward democracy and individualism and a new moral self-confidence in Western European man—new because it is based, for the first time, on something like philosophical argument rather than religious convictions. It is thus bolder, more universal and more directly and frankly forward-looking, and linked more closely and comfortably with the new enlightenment, with the belief that man's moral powers will be further heightened by the development of education and science, freeing him from bondage and superstition.

III

Edmund Burke, who had so strongly supported the aspirations of the American colonists, rejected 'these metaphysic rights' of the French Revolution: he believed that they illegitimately abstracted the individual from society, cast men adrift from the moorings of history and tradition and put irresponsibility and arbitrary authority in place of the sober judgment of and serious involvement in the affairs of state that rested on the great estates of the realm. Jeremy Bentham, too, thought that the French declarations were 'a perpetual vein of nonsense, flowing from a perpetual abuse of words', that they showed 'the acts of the Senate loaded and disfigured by the tinsel of the playhouse'. Contracts, he insisted, in his essay *Anarchical Fallacies*, come from government and not government from contracts; there are no rights before and outside society. '*Natural rights* is simple nonsense: natural and imprescriptible rights, rhetorical nonsense— nonsense upon stilts.' In so far as Bentham is making a logical point, denying that such rights can be empirically or 'scientifically' established, he is right. For 'natural' or 'human' rights belong to the difficult, often vague and confused, class of *moral* rights, where one often feels that anything goes, and not to the positive, empirical category of legal or customary rights, rights whose existence is established by inspecting actual, historical legal arrangements, codes and decisions or past and existing customs and traditions.

To preach morality is easy, to give ethics a foundation is difficult. In traditional moral philosophy, as in popular moralism and moral parlance today, the subject-matter of ethics and the nature of moral demands or prescriptions were confused and obscured in the illogical concept of a normative science or set of normative truths, in the attempt to give ethical judgments and moral demands the objectivity of scientific descriptions as well as the imperative, exhortative force sought by proposals, prohibitions, recommendations and commands. Moral philosophy, in short, paralleled the fraudulence of everyday moral language and commands; it presented as impartial what was partial, as desir*able* what was merely desir*ed*. This appeared most patently in those moral philosophers, and those glib speakers of the English language or other languages, who treated the word 'good' as meaning 'that whose nature requires that it be commended and pursued'. But if the function of morality, like that of legislation, is to *prescribe* then it can be concerned only with situations in which it is possible for people to behave in different ways. If the nature of man or of anything else dictated certain modes of behaviour as gravitational laws 'dictate' the behaviour of falling bodies, moral and legal prescription would be pointless. We do not tell a man that he ought to do that which he cannot help doing. If the *ius naturale* or the *Tao* or the dictates of conscience, the moral sense, or practical reason were laws that bind as the laws of nature bind there would be no point in exhorting or commanding anyone to follow them. Men have exhorted or commanded obedience to moral and to legal norms precisely because these norms are not part of, and do not simply follow from, 'the nature of things', because there are no universal ends or standards that all men *must* follow.

If moral philosophy, or 'moral science' is concerned to guide action, if its content is a set of 'principles'—that is, commendations, prescriptions, demands, commands or requirements—then we have to recognize that the moral predicates are in fact *relations*. But relations require at least *two* terms—the demander as well as the demanded, the pursuer as well as the pursued, the obliger as well as the obliged. What is made obligatory or demanded by one code, moral tradition or person may be forbidden or rejected by another. The concept of absolute obligation of unconditional codes and duties is thus revealed as a contradiction in terms, while the illusion of a single binding morality has to be replaced by the empirical recognition of competing 'principles', 'authorities' and ways of life, in other words, of competing traditions, demands and codes that cannot be brought before a common tribunal or under an 'ultimate' law. The relational character of moral terms like 'right' and 'wrong' is evident; what is right in terms of one morality may be wrong in terms of another. Similarly, what are 'rights' under one morality—for example, the 'right' to dissolve a marriage or to have an abortion—are not under another. The moralist has an interest in preventing this recognition; he requires both the imperative force and the vagueness of terms like 'right' and 'wrong' and the suggestion of absolute, unconditional, qualitative distinctions conveyed by the terms 'good' and 'bad'.

The normative function of moralism has partly depended on the adoption of a moral language particularly suited to obscuring the sources of the demands it makes by dealing in incomplete relations. 'You ought to do this', 'Stealing is wrong', 'Children must obey their elders', all suggest authority without specifying it: in many cases they thus successfully invoke the terrors of an anonymous authority, or of one filled in by the hearer himself, simply by leaving the relation incomplete. Ethical discussion and enquiry, on the other hand, require the completion of the relation and thus threaten the foundations of moral obedience much as a close acquaintance with officers and the general staff threatens the foundations of military obedience. It is here that the moralist is driven back on hierarchical, anti-empirical, conceptions of reality. If ethical propositions are to have prescriptive force, the source of moral demands must be elevated above 'the world' to which the demands are addressed. It is thus that the relational, prescriptive treatment of 'good' readily leads moralists to a dualism of 'facts' and 'standards', 'actions' and 'principles', 'apparent interests' and 'true interests'. This is patently obvious where the source of moral obligation is treated as supra-empirical, as god, soul, or an unhistorical faculty of reason or conscience. It is equally true, however, where the source is allegedly 'natural'—'natural' law, human nature, human interests, social demands or the 'original' social contract. These, too, have to be given a primacy in which moral advocacy masquerades as logical priority and is left imprecise to avoid conflict and incoherence. It is here that we find the reappearance of constitutive relations to protect the source of moral authority from criticism. Just as 'conscience' becomes that whose nature it is to approve of good, so 'principles' become that whose nature it is to be obeyed. For the social and historical investigation of moral attitudes, we find substituted the attempt to bind conduct with tautologies.

The doctrine of natural or human rights, then, is not an empirical description of the consequences implied by an actually existing law of nature, essential or common humanity or historical social contract. The attempt, at various stages in the history of the doctrine, to appeal to these was scientifically fraudulent and remains so. The doctrine of human rights is a *proposal* concerning the morally appropriate way of treating men and organizing society. Like all such proposals that gain force and command respect, it is a complex proposal, attempting to present a systematic view of man and society, taking up associated empirical material, relating and ordering moral preferences. It is to be judged by its internal coherence and logical consistency, by the truth of its associated empirical claims and its relation to relevant empirical material that it may or may not take up and, in the last resort, by its relation and that of its consequences and implications to our own moral beliefs. The reader will find in this volume a particularly careful and systematic elaboration of such a proposal of how we should treat persons in society in the contribution of Mr Benn; but he will also learn from the contributions of Mr Arnold, Dr Kleinig and Professor Wellman, and from the attitudes and beliefs described by Professor Tay, that other systematic moral views are possible, that Mr Benn's respect for persons may stand in some tension with such moral doctrines as utilitarianism, the elevation of welfare, of group rights or of social equality. Above all, he may find in this volume further evidence that rights may well live at each other's expense and that it is not only difficult to give ethics a foundation, but even more difficult to render a moral system or a society free of conflict and what Marxists call 'contradictions'—competing and logically irreconcilable preferences and demands that nevertheless depend on each other.

2

Natural rights, ideology and the game of life

K. R. Minogue

I Divergent views of human emancipation

In 1789, the French revolutionaries summed up what they regarded as the essence of human emancipation in the Declaration of the Rights of Man. This declaration was not just an exercise in moral and political theory: it was a programme of action designed to sweep away the cobwebs of feudalism. More than that, it was a whole philosophy of what it was to be a human being. But emancipation was not to be contained in the formulations of one generation, and in 1843 Karl Marx wrote that 'the so-called *rights of man*, the *droits de l'homme* as distinct from the *droits du citoyen*, are nothing but the rights of a *member of civil society*, that is, the rights of egoistic man, of man separated from other men and from the community.'[1] Marx's objection was not merely to the lists of rights which became so fashionable at the end of the eighteenth century: it was rather to the very notion of rights at all. Rights, Marx believed, imply the separation of man from man, while his own conception of revolutionary emancipation envisaged the union of man with man—a union that was social rather than legal and political. What is at issue between these two versions of human emancipation?

The French revolutionaries conceived the defect of the *ancien régime* as lying in the invasion, by the arbitrary practices of the Bourbon absolute monarchy, of the space in which a man might live his own life. Declarations of rights, therefore, were prohibitions of such invasion. Each man, in exercising his natural rights, could enjoy his own household free from the threat of arbitrary arrest; he could practice his own religion (or none); he could buy and sell property without interference from a grasping and despotic state. Marx believed this account of the evils of feudalism to be fundamentally erroneous. The

[1] Karl Marx, 'On the Jewish Question' in Karl Marx and Frederick Engels, *Collected Works* III (London, 1975), p. 162.

right of property, the liberty to buy and sell freely, he argued, actually involved a situation in which some men (whom he called the bourgeoisie) would enslave the persons and expropriate the work of large numbers of others (whom he called the proletariat). One kind of undesirable invasion was thus being cured only by facilitating a different and in some ways even more intolerable invasion of human autonomy. The question of human emancipation needed to be understood in terms quite other than the individualist idea of natural rights.

This lively and continuing dispute is of philosophical interest because the complex and unfolding shifts of political controversy continually obscure the conceptual boundaries in terms of which it may be understood. Modern politics, for example, is often discussed in terms of ideas like 'human rights' and 'social rights'; the shift from one adjective to another may plausibly but erroneously be seen as constituting merely tactical attempts to blur the boundaries of the dispute for the politician's purpose of gaining support. The dispute is also of vibrant practical interest because the way we *formulate* how we live influences the way we do live in important respects. This, of course, is a well trodden field. One powerful strand of thought suggests that Marx, by using the resources of Hegelian philosophy and exhibiting the historicity of earlier conceptions of human emancipation, revealed the limiting abstractness of natural rights doctrine. Natural rights for Marx are statements of the demands of the bourgeoisie and of the necessary conditions of capitalist enterprise. Another strand of thought—*contra* Marx—points to the despotic consequences likely to follow from abandoning a concern for individual natural rights, and argues that Marx lost sight of human emancipation by pursuing a will-o'-the-wisp of absolute liberty. There are few controversies in modern politics which cannot be accommodated within the framework of these ideas.

The dispute is, above all, a dispute about the character of human life, and I have chosen to focus it on the ideas of rights and of ideology. Both ideas present well known difficulties. In the next two sections I shall be discussing the idea of rights, partly historically and partly analytically. The term 'ideology' has difficulties all its own. It is used in so many divergent ways that many people prefer to abandon it altogether. It may, for example, be used to cover any statement of what is politically or socially desirable. If it were understood in this sense, my whole argument would have to be reformulated, because natural rights, being political desirabilities, would themselves be ideological. If this objection were to be pressed hard, then the subject of this essay would be the incompatability between the individualist ideology of natural rights and the collectivist ideologies of social involvement. For reasons that will emerge, this would be historically muddled: the belief in political rights can and does constitute a critique of ideological thinking, a critique of utopianism; but this would not at all affect the analytical point of my argument. The issue is not about the use of words, but about the way people actually live.

II The character of natural rights

Our central problem is to lay bare the connection between natural rights and ideology. We have seen that Marx is hostile to the whole idea of natural rights, and we have generalized this into the suggestion that all ideologies are hostile to the idea of natural rights. The experience of anarchist, nationalist, fascist and other thought and action confirms that such antipathy is usually to be found among ideologists. There can be no place for rights in a purportedly perfect society. But the clue to any essential antipathy between the two ideas requires that we should analyse further the meaning of 'natural rights'. Why did the very expression itself come to have such widespread currency from the seventeenth century onwards and, just as interesting, why did it largely go out of fashion in the nineteenth century?

There are, I suggest, a cluster of false leads that must first be cleared out of our way. The central false lead is that which derives natural rights from the longer and grander tradition of natural law thinking.[2] The plausibility of this widespread opinion cannot be denied. What could be more obvious than that a law should generate rights? And where could a natural right come from except from a natural law, something widely asserted and deeply entrenched in Western thought since medieval times? Did not the philosophy of natural law flourish on the Continent at the same time as natural rights were being asserted in England and elsewhere? Did not John Locke, the only philosopher of any distinction to employ the idea of natural rights, also write a series of essays on the law of nature? Can we not trace many of his ideas back through Hooker to the Scholastic tradition of Aquinas?

This and more might correctly be asserted to support the common view of the matter. What it does show conclusively is that the plausibility of natural rights doctrine was parasitic upon its better established and more respectable relation. But the first thing to make us pause before regarding natural rights as a by-product of natural law is the fact that virtually all the exponents of natural rights tended to be publicists and polemicists with little knowledge of the natural law

---

[2] For example, Margaret Macdonald in 'Natural Rights', *Proceedings of the Aristotelian Society* n.s. XLVII (1946–7), pp. 225–50, identifies the two traditions in terms of their common allegiance to nature and so, with some caution, does D. G. Ritchie in *Natural Rights* (London, 1894). Leo Strauss, *Natural Right and History* (Chicago, 1953) takes quite a different view.

tradition. The main exception to this is, of course, John Locke, but the *Second Treatise*, as is now widely recognized, is not at all what it seems.[3] It is a political polemic couched in philosophical language, and will not bear much weight as evidence of the connection. It shows that John Locke believed both in natural rights and in natural law; it will not show that they are part and parcel of the same fundamental belief.

Let us descend from these comparative heights and consider two statements much more typical of how the idea of natural rights was commonly employed. One is from the beginning of its pre-eminence (1646) and the other from near its end (1791):

> To every Individual in nature, is given an individual property by nature, not to be invaded or usurped by any: for every one as he is himself, so he hath a Self propriety, else could he not be himself, and on this no second may presume to deprive any of, without manifest violation and affront to the very principles of nature.[4]

and later:

> Natural rights are those which appertain to man in right of his existence. Of this kind are all the intellectual rights, or rights of the mind, and also all those rights of acting as an individual for his own comfort and happiness, which are not injurious to the natural rights of others.[5]

Here are two relatively uneducated men talking about liberty and using what they imagine to be an impressive and classical vocabulary, in both cases more or less unnecessarily, to state their case. Natural rights may best be understood as the statement of an argument for liberty, often for a particular set of liberties, rhetorically expressed in what looked at the time like a technical language. The proponents of natural rights wish to put the desirability of certain liberties beyond the ups and downs of political deliberations and positive law. The currency of natural law made its vocabulary a convenient one for political use, even though this use was often at variance with the main drift of natural law theory itself.

These historical considerations may be reinforced if we turn to the actual logic of the idea of a right. It is commonly taken for granted that rights and duties are correlative. Thus E. F. Carritt talks of 'duties and the corresponding rights',[6] and Maurice Cranston more cautiously

---

[3] See Peter Laslett's introduction to John Locke, *Two Treatises of Government: a Critical Edition* (Cambridge, 1960), p. 45.

[4] Richard Overton, *An Arrow Against All Tyrants*, a facsimile reprint of the first edition of 1646 (Exeter, 1976), p. 1.

[5] Thomas Paine, *The Rights of Man*, part 1, Everyman's Library (London, 1906, reprinted 1954), p. 44.

[6] E. F. Carritt, *Ethical and Political Thinking* (Oxford, 1947), p. 155.

tells us that 'rights bear a clear relationship to duties.'[7] Certainly, this is the most common sort of relationship between rights and duties, especially where these are the abstract terms in which are described the roles men take up when they cooperate. A ruler has the right to command laws, while the subject has to obey; correspondingly, the subject has a right to justice and protection which it is the duty of the ruler to provide. The rational principle by which these moral relations are explained and justified is the end or point of the association. Reciprocity is both the end and the law of human cooperation. Similar considerations apply to armies, marriages, universities and any other form of human cooperation which may be described in terms of the metaphor of an organism. They also apply to contracts of partnership and to economic exchange. Taking our lead from these central cases of the reciprocity of rights and duties, it may seem obvious that we ought to construe my right to life, liberty and property in terms of your duty not to interfere with my life, liberty and property.

Natural law and natural rights are merely different ways of saying the same thing. Natural rights is an assertive and individualistic version of what appears in the bland and urbane philosophy of natural law as an elaborate and compendious account of human moral obligations. The one is the voice of the wise governor explaining how everything fits together, while the other is the shrill self-assertiveness of the moralizing subordinate—and sometimes, insubordinate. And since an obligation may be specified more precisely than a right (and English law has sensibly evolved remedies rather than rights), it might seem that the doctrine of natural rights is merely an intellectually misjudged but usefully rhetorical formulation of what is better put in terms of natural law. But the actual situation is inevitably more complicated than an attention to the paradigmatic uses of rights and duties might suggest, and my argument is that it is the exceptions rather than the model itself which throw most light upon the character of natural rights.

For one thing, the idea of natural rights does not belong purely to the vocabulary of moral thought. The area in which its expression has had its most explosive influence is in politics. It seems to me that something has been left out by construing natural rights in this way, and that we may best discover this uncultivated area if we direct our attention to those features of the expression 'right' where the correlative relation with duty is absent. The literature of natural rights has of late been much preoccupied with them.

There are, for example, plenty of cases where I have a duty towards someone who has no rights against me. I have a duty (moral, if not legal) to try to rescue a drowning man, at least when there is no possible

[7] 'Human Rights, Real and Supposed' in D. D. Raphael, editor, *Political Theory and the Rights of Man* (London, 1967), p. 50.

danger to myself, but this person does not have a corresponding right to have me save him. A code like the Ten Commandments imposes upon me the duty of not killing my fellow man, without thereby according to him a right to life. In general, duty and obligation are terms of much wider application than right in moral discourse, and 'rights' are, therefore, but limited and ill-defined shadows of them. A world in which all duties were precisely the reflection of rights would be an accountant's world, a place with no room for the higher reaches of moral experience and for what theologians call 'works of supererogation'.

Let us now turn to the other side of this particular coin—the case of rights that do not involve duties. The most famous case of a right that does not imply an obligation is the Hobbesian right of nature.[8] Man in the Hobbesian state of nature is not morally obliged to refrain from *any* act that he judges necessary for his survival; but the right that he possesses in no way casts any shadow of obligation upon his fellows, each of whom is in the same position. The moral world of correlative rights and duties in principle dovetails rights into obligations and means that, in a virtuous world where everybody performed his duties, everyone would at least enjoy his rights. There is no such dovetailing in the Hobbesian state of nature and it takes the sovereign to produce the necessary reciprocities between rights and duties in a system of law.

Or let us consider a similar but wider type of case for which Herbert Hart provides our example. 'Two people walking along both see a ten dollar bill in the road twenty yards away, and there is no clue as to the owner. Neither of the two are [*sic*] under a "duty" to allow the other to pick it up; each has in this sense a right to pick it up. Of course there may be many things which each has a "duty" not to do in the course of the race to the spot—neither may kill or wound the other—and corresponding to these "duties" there are rights to forbearances. The moral propriety of all economic competition implies this minimum sense of "a right" in which to say that "*X* has a right to" means merely that *X* is under no "duty" not to.'[9] Hart points out that jurists have isolated rights in this sense and have called them 'liberties'.

Consider just one more example. When we describe the structure of roles in a game, we are concerned with rights that have no correlative duties. The goalkeeper has a right to pick up the football with his hands and he may do so in defending the goal, but 'this liberty to do or forbear' (as Hobbes would call it) in no way imposes a duty upon any one else involved in the game. Again, a squash player has the right to a second service if the first one goes out, but no duty is directly involved.

[8] Thomas Hobbes, *Leviathan*, part I, chapter 14.
[9] H. L. A. Hart, 'Are There any Natural Rights', *Philosophical Review* LXIV (1955), pp. 175–91 at p. 179.

These cases all provoke my interest because their logic corresponds to what I regard as a significant feature of the rhetoric of rights in political discussion. And this feature is the fact that the rhetorical partner of a 'right' in politics is not a duty, but simply an absence of right or, as we might say for convenience, 'a non-right'.[10] What corresponds to 'I have a right to do X' is not 'you have a duty to let me do X' but 'you have no right to stop me from doing X', where the emphasis in the sentence may fall on the 'you' or on the 'right' according to the point that is being made, and where the correspondence tells us not what is logically implied but what would appropriately be said. It would positively mislead our understanding if we were to mistake this absence of a right for an actual duty. It is nothing of the sort.

Now, to follow the contours of this difficult matter, we need to distinguish between what I shall call 'uniting' rights and what I shall call 'separating' rights. A uniting right defines the boundaries at which two roles come together; it indicates the proper connection between them and it may appropriately be described in terms of reciprocal rights and duties. When I go into the shop and buy something, the shopkeeper and I each have our respective rights and duties which define the whole in which we participate, a 'whole' which may be called a purchase or a transaction. And a similar symbiosis is to be found in the relations of ruler and ruled, lord and vassal, husband and wife— and parents and children. Take this last case, in which the parents owe protection and guidance and the children owe respect and obedience. This is an interesting case, because there have been societies in which this particular relationship has been construed not in terms of reciprocity of rights and duties but in terms of ownership of property. Children belonged to the parents, specifically to the father, and his *patria potestas* was absolute. These days, the family is construed as both a moral and a legal arena and the children are accorded rights protecting them against the brutality of some parents. And it is significant that this shift in our moral understanding moves towards the attribution of what I have called 'separating rights'. Consider, for example, a more or less typical statement from a newspaper report:

Children no longer belonged to their parents like a pair of shoes, Professor C. Henry Kempe told the Conference on Battered Children in Perth last year.

Children belonged to themselves and had certain rights to protection from neglect and cruelty, even when this meant protection from their parents, the US pediatrician said.

The 'separateness' of children was recognized globally when the

[10] Cf. the notion of a 'no-right' in W. N. Hohfeld's *Fundamental Legal Conceptions* (New Haven, 1919).

United Nations drew up the Declaration of the Rights of the Child in 1959.[11]

Such rights for children may not be 'rights' in a sense that Professor Hart would approve, because he thinks, very plausibly, that rights should be a particular sub-class of the general range of things we *ought* to do, and that the best test of a right is some precedent act which creates it.[12] But they clearly are conceivable as rights in the political sense that I have been discussing, and they seem to me to illustrate the truth of Marx's remark: 'But the right of man to liberty is based not on the association of man with man, but on the separation of man from man'.[13] To call the rights I am concerned with here 'separating' rights thus seems to accord with a widespread perception of their special character.

The distinction between uniting and separating rights rests not upon the content of the rights but upon the way in which they are conceived. There is a right to property in both Aquinas and Locke, but in the case of Aquinas the right unites the owner of the property with his fellow men by way of the duties of charity and succour of the needy,[14] whereas the Lockean right to property is a 'separating' right because no duties directly attach to it.[15] To develop the character of the distinction further, we need to incorporate into our understanding the political fact that natural rights were almost invariably conceived of as rights *against* the government. Rights, *pace* H. J. McCloskey,[16] are always, I think, rights *against* some outside threat, and historically they have been most commonly, though not invariably, directed against governments.[17] The attitude of political philosophers to absolute government in the seventeenth and eighteenth centuries was usually coloured by their image of despotism, an image clearly expressed by a sixteenth-century Venetian ambassador to the Grand Turk:

[11] *Sydney Morning Herald*, Wednesday 7 July 1976, p. 24.

[12] Hart, *op. cit.*

[13] Marx and Engels, *op. cit.*, p. 162.

[14] Thomas Aquinas, *Summa Theologica*, Qu. 66 in his *Selected Political Writings*, edited by A. P. d'Entrèves (Oxford, 1948), p. 169: 'Men should not hold material things as their own, but to the common benefit: each readily sharing them with others in their necessity.'

[15] John Locke, *The Second Treatise of Government*, chapter 5, cf. his *Two Treatises, op. cit.*, pp. 303–20. There are of course *limits*, and we may suggest that duties correspond to uniting rights, and limits to separating rights.

[16] H. J. McCloskey, 'Rights', *Philosophical Quarterly* xv (1965), pp. 115–27 at p. 118: 'My right to life is not a right against anyone.' I find this puzzling, since it would seem odd to talk about a *right* to life unless the matter were in some sort of doubt.

[17] Hobbes in *Leviathan* and John Stuart Mill in *On Liberty* clearly envisage threats coming from other people rather than governments. And both are clearly thinking in terms of a secure space in which the individual may live his life.

When someone dies, the Grand Signor, who is the real owner of everything, takes whatever he wants from the estate, and considers it a favour if he leaves anything to the widow and the children. He can easily find pretexts to make it appear that justice requires him to confiscate the goods. He often takes property from the wealthy, a thing he can easily do because no one would dare to speak out against him. The mere will of the Grand Signor is justification enough to do anything in the world.[18]

It is against such a picture of arbitrary power, as provoked by matters like ship-money and the *lettres de cachet*, that assertions of natural rights were made, and hence it seems plausible to construe their real meaning in terms of a claim to a secured *space* in which subjects might pursue their own concerns without interference from the powers that be.

The idea of rights in this early modern period, then, was a way of talking about liberty which attempted to entrench particularly valued liberties in the nature of man and thus to render them less vulnerable to the ups and downs of political pressure. But such an aspiration is concerned with more than what we may, with memories of such spatial images as that 'an Englishman's house is his castle' in our minds, call 'political houseroom'. Bearers of uniting rights and those of separating rights are different in character. Uniting rights concern themselves with the playing of roles—parents, purchasers, rulers, governors and so on. Separating rights on the other hand imply a complete individual, by which is meant someone who is a rational agent, and who has a determinate set of desires and aspirations to be the materials of his rational agency. In saying this, I am, of course, merely repeating the oft-told tale of the emergence of the modern world: the rest of this section will consist of a redescription of this well known story.

The idea of an independent individual pursuing his own self-generated purposes has often been taken as an implausible account of human beings, because they are more realistically to be understood as the creatures of their society, framing purposes they draw from its traditions in a language they inherit from its collective creativity. This kind of criticism has often been used against the social contract theory, but it is, of course, largely beside the point. Like any other account of social and political life, the argument of natural rights takes much for granted, and it seems to me that we may understand it a little better if we consider just what is or is not here being taken for granted. The idea of the modern individual has often been understood as the self-assertion of a particular social class; individualism is the character of the bourgeois. It has sometimes been understood in patriarchal

[18] *Pursuit of Power: Venetian Ambassadors' Reports on Spain, Turkey and France in the Age of Philip II, 1560–1600*, edited and translated by James C. Davis (New York, 1970), p. 143. This report is by Gianfrancesco Morosini.

terms.[19] But it seems to me that it can best be interpreted as a generalization of what is involved in the activity of governing. In 1531, Sir Thomas Elyot wrote a book of advice for the responsible classes of England. It was called *The Book named The Governor*,[20] and the term he used for the kind of activity he had in mind survived as a kind of title in English usage up until quite recent times, often in the familiar term of 'guv'. A governor is someone set in authority ('set in a high place' is the expression Elyot uses) and responsible for the ordering of some activity. These are people who 'nothing do acquire by the said influence of knowledge for their own necessities, but do employ all the powers of their wits and their diligence to the only preservation of other their inferiors'.[21] Governors are a highly miscellaneous class of person, including not only princes and magistrates, but military officers, ambassadors, owners of commercial enterprises, royal ministers, schoolmasters and so on. Elyot tends to understand governors as a kind of class of the realm to be contrasted with those who lack eminence, but he certainly does not construe them narrowly as being a social class. The general principle on which he operates would allow almost everyone to see himself, in one sphere or another, as a kind of governor. We are all, in fact, both governors and governed, and my interpretation of Locke's famous remark, 'Each person hath a property in his own person', is to see it in just this way. It seems worth considering the view that the doctrine of natural rights expresses the assertiveness of those who identify themselves in this particular manner.

A governor, as Elyot sees him, is someone who owes duties to those whose activities he directs. His relations with his inferiors are fundamentally cooperative. But his relations with other governors of the same kind may very well be competitive. This is certainly the case with the relations between sovereign princes as they pursue mutual antipathies and alliances; it is notoriously true of commercial entrepreneurs. But it may also be true of fathers of families seeking to keep up with the Joneses, of schoolmasters with different views of education or, indeed, anyone else. It is not true that such equals cannot cooperate, and they often do so, but it is only by a voluntary mitigation of the rights that attach to them as governors.

Given such a situation, we may identify as the governor's crux in life the conflict between his pursuing his own possibly competitive purposes in life in relation to his own circle on the one hand and, at the

[19] Cf. Peter Laslett's introduction to Sir Robert Filmer, *Patriarcha and other Political Works* (Oxford, 1949), pp. 20–33.

[20] Sir Thomas Elyot, *The Book named The Governor*, Everyman's Library (London, 1907, reprinted 1962). Among the many splendid modern echoes of the book is the beginning of I, 15: 'Lord God, how many good and clean wits of children be nowadays perished by ignorant schoolmasters!'

[21] *ibid.*, p. 5.

same time, performing his duties to his prince or other superior on the other. So far as the prince himself is concerned, the independent activities of these subordinate governors may well be impediments to the order which he seeks to impose, as when the strength he requires from his kingdom for war is being dissipated by internal dissensions or by such practices as duelling. To a governor, and particularly a prince, looking down at those to whose activities he brings order, the obvious picture of the world is that contained in the philosophy of natural law. It is a network of harmonizing duties. To a governor, however, who is thinking in terms of his relations with equals, and indeed even with superiors, the natural picture of a desirable structure of rules is the one asserted by the doctrine of natural rights.

Here, then, is one more version of that commonplace of politics, the conflict between the governors and the governed. But why, we may ask, should there be any conflict at all? Why can life not actually be lived in accordance with that harmonious structure of rules which were elaborated by the natural lawyers of medieval and later times? At one level the answer might be in terms of pride and original sin; at another in terms of the divergent interests of individuals and groups. There is much to be said in favour of both these suggestions, but I wish to ignore them in favour of exploring one form of the conflict which has been much less thoroughly discussed. This is the view that governors are playing games. And, as will become clear, I mean by this much more than a mere metaphor.

III Natural rights and the rules of the game

Imagine a man who goes out to shoot a deer so as to provision himself for the next week or more. Various rules or considerations will affect his behaviour. He must approach up wind, and work mostly at dawn and dusk, in stalking his prey. Thus far, we might as easily be describing any competent organism, since a reasonably intelligent tiger would behave in much the same way, though he might not be doing so in response to rules. We leave the organism behind, and begin to describe a man, only when we turn to other sorts of rules that might arise for our hunter to consider. If he is a religious man, he may have to look at the calendar in order not to find himself profaning the sabbath. If he is a law-abiding member of the community, there will be legal rules to consider, such as whether it is now the hunting season. If he is a moral man he may ponder his action and decide that he must subscribe to rules about only killing where it is necessary for food, and then only in an efficient way that minimizes pain to the deer. Here then is a collection of some of the main types of rules which complicate the simple purposiveness of human beings. As the judicious Hooker writes:

Only Man's observation of the Law of his Nature is Righteousness, only Man's transgression Sin. And the reason of this is the difference in his manner of observing or transgressing the Law of his Nature. He doth not otherwise than voluntarily the one or the other.[22]

Now it is true that many changes may be rung on this traditional schema of man's voluntary relation to law. Attempts have been made to reduce these types of rule to some kind of single impulse. A utilitarian may be inclined to see man as a satisfaction-seeking creature to whose complex purposes complex technical considerations apply. All except the technical rules may be regarded as a repressive hangover from the superstitions and class divisiveness of hitherto existing societies; or the whole scheme may be criticized as a practical abstraction from the concrete situation in which the complex nature of man expresses itself in an outcome of behaviour. But whatever qualifications one might wish to advance, I think that this picture of human life is at the very least plausible enough as far as it goes; and I wish to add to it by referring to a further source of rules which affect our huntsman.

If he is a twentieth-century huntsman, he may take the view that there is something wrong about shooting a deer with a high-powered modern rifle; and since he is not in immediate need of food (or even perhaps if he is) he may impose further rules on himself, for instance, that the deer is only to be shot with a bow and arrow, or that it may only be shot from a distance such that it becomes a test of skill. The more rules our huntsman becomes subject to, the more difficulty he will have in accommodating them. Those rules requiring special skill, for example, run the risk of conflict with the rule that the deer should be killed with the minimum of pain. One part of moral philosophy is, of course, concerned with ways of solving this kind of problem. But this I leave to one side. What interests me more here is the question of what kind of rules those are, which I have just mentioned.

One possible way of understanding such rules is in terms of personal honour, but this is to construe the rule in terms of its presumed source rather than in terms of its general character. And the rules we impose on ourselves for reasons of honour may vary greatly in character. Some will simply be moral rules honourably enforced, such as 'I am not the sort of person who steals.' Others may be aesthetic: 'It is unbecoming to lose one's dignity by rushing merely to be at the head of the queue.' Still others may be the most exiguous children of pride: 'I don't let *my* garden get into a mess'. Hence, while honour may be the source of such rules as I am considering, it is neither necessary nor sufficient in causing them to arise. But in the case of the deer hunter, it is obvious

[22] Richard Hooker, *Of The Laws of Ecclesiastical Polity*, books 1–5, Everyman's Library (2 vols, London, 1907) I, p. 186.

that the additional rule turns the activity into sport, or a game. And gaming here may describe both the *source* of the rule, since it refers to an original human propensity, and also the *character* of the rule, since it transforms what is going on in a special way. Usually our hunter will be engaging both in the purposive activity of hunting, and the gaming activity of enjoying a test of his skill, but there may well be a conflict between these two activities, and either of them may be separately pursued.

The disposition to turn human activities into games is very strong and has often been discussed. The most single-minded exposition of it as a human propensity is, I suppose, that of the Dutch historian Johan Huizinga in his *Homo Ludens*.[23] Modern philosophers, becoming preoccupied with man as a rule-following creature, have found the idea of a game so suitable to their purposes that they have recently, and perhaps rightly, been accused of overdoing it.[24] But my concern is not to continue the excessive use of an example, nor to construe the whole of human life in ludic terms, but to point to what I take to be a real impulse in human beings, one which generates rules and forms of behaviour, and one that seems to be relevant to understanding modern natural rights.

The point is that people do not only play games in a separate sphere of life called 'leisure', but that they are capable of turning absolutely anything into a game. They play games with themselves, as when they try to walk along the footpaths without stepping on the cracks of the paving stones. The commonest games, no doubt, are played between individuals or groups. And the commonest way in which any activity turns into a game is by the springing into existence of a spirit of competition, in which people recognize themselves to be competitors. Such a move immediately brings about a set of implicit rules forbidding moves that would invalidate the point of the game. A group of men digging holes in the ground can move from the *purposive* to the *gaming* by deciding to compete for who is going to be the first to finish. Shooting one's competitor is clearly not a way of winning the game, being forbidden by an implicit rule following from the point of the game as a contest of skill and energy. Two competing armies are affected by rules of a game if one of them refuses the possibility of a successful surprise attack and draws itself up on the plain so as to have a fair battle with its opponent. Often technically necessary arrangements, such as examinations, will almost automatically turn an activity into a game.

Pure games, at one end of the scale, have no outside point at all.

---

[23] J. Huizinga, *Homo Ludens: a Study of the Play Element in Culture* (London and New York, 1970), originally published in German in 1944. Cf. also Roger Caillois, *Les Jeux et Les Hommes*, édition revue (Paris, 1958).

[24] Mary Midgley, 'The Game Game', *Philosophy* XLIX (1974), pp. 231–53.

They may well involve chance without any addition of skill, as in ludo and some card games. The better games do involve skill, and skill can be further divided into the mastery of technique combined with a sense of tactics and strategy. At the other end of the scale, purely purposive activities like baking a cake, earning a living, digging a ditch and so on are governed by moral and technical rules but need involve no element of gaming. Competition is the bridge that may introduce an element of gaming, though it need not do so. It is possible to think of many situations in which people compete for some scarce object, and the point of their activities is *merely* to get the object. But in human life, this is rare. Almost always, the person who gets the object not only attains his purpose but also enjoys the satisfaction of winning against an opponent. It will be obvious that such glorying in victory is morally ambiguous; indeed, winning the competition may itself become a kind of purpose for a competitor. Hence competition must be seen neither as a necessary nor as a sufficient condition of gaming. The real point of gaming lies in testing oneself on a specific occasion in a specific respect against the skill of an opponent; in true gaming, one plays against his skill and his luck rather than against the competitor himself. It is possible to treat the whole of life as a kind of grand game in which one explores one's skill and capabilities in relation to one's fellow men.[25] In these terms, one's obituary is a kind of sporting commentary. The game of life would, of course, be quite intolerable if there were only a single game in which everyone participated. Human beings, however, have so constructed their world that there is an enormous variety of games to be played, reflecting the enormous number of capacities human beings have found in themselves; it has further been constructed so that winning one version of the game is actually logically incompatible with winning other versions. The successful businessman may be construed as a spiritual failure just because he has succeeded in business; the boy on whom every educational advantage has been showered has almost certainly lost his proletarian authenticity. All experienced gamesters recognize that 'you can't win 'em all'. This agonistic—some would say agonizing—view of life is not, of course, new. It will be remembered that Hobbes construed life as a race. 'But this *race* we must suppose to have no other *goal*, nor other *garland*, but being foremost, and in it.'[26] Hobbes admits that the parallel is not exact, and certainly, stated in this bald fashion, life appears somewhat more grim than it is commonly experienced. What is

[25] Thus Adam Ferguson noted that 'The Stoics conceived human life under the image of a Game; at which the entertainment and merit of the players consisted in playing attentively and well, whether the stake was great or small.' *Principles of Moral and Political Science* (2 vols, Edinburgh, 1792), part I, introduction, p. 7.

[26] *Human Nature*, chapter 9, section 21, quoted from T. Hobbes, *Body, Man and Citizen*: selections edited by R. S. Peters (New York, 1962), p. 224.

missing from it is something he recognizes elsewhere—a certain scorn of merely winning in an inglorious fashion, something he takes to be real, though rare.[27] This element may be understood as personal honour and in this form it plays an important part in the self-understanding produced by exponents of Anglo-Saxon politics and amateur sport. The ferocities resulting from the corruption of winning as a result of a purposive attitude may be mitigated not merely by a sense of honour, but also by a direct propensity to have a sense of what a game is about. This sense is to be found diffused through all the activities of life.

That the contrast between directly purposive activity and playing the game is a common way of understanding the human situation seems to me hard to deny. Thus a farmer commenting upon the drought of 1976 in Britain remarked, 'That is something you have to expect in farming . . . It is part of the game',[28] while Edward Heath has said:

> I came into politics to try to achieve certain objectives, and when you are out of office then you have no direct power to try to achieve anything at all . . . If you are in politics because it is a game, or because you like to have a front seat in the stalls or because you just enjoy arguing with other people, well then you can carry on in Opposition in much the same way. That has never been of interest to me because I saw all too many things which required to be done and wanted to take some part in doing them.[29]

In life, as in politics, one may play a game, or get things done, or perhaps both.

What happens when 'getting things done' is modified by an element of gaming? One consequence is that we must think in terms of an additional set of rules. A technical problem, which involves manipulating material, is replaced by a completely different set of considerations. The purpose of getting power at all costs, moderated only by a wariness about the long-term dangers of going to extremes, is replaced by an activity in which keeping to the rules of the game is more important than actually winning. The effect of construing party politics either as prudence or as gaming is often so similar as to be almost indistinguishable, but the difference is vital. For the prudent calculation, 'If I destroy my opponents, others may come along and later destroy me', may as easily be replaced by the equally rational calculation, 'If I do *not* destroy my opponents, they may well in time destroy me.' The conception of long-term interest is thus inadequate in explaining the self-restraint of a properly functioning system of competing parties, whereas the notion that they are, in a significant

[27] *Leviathan*, part I, chapter 15.
[28] *The Times*, 18 September 1976, p. 3.
[29] *The Times*, 23 August 1976, p. 5.

way, playing politics as a game does correspond to the reality. (This point was clearly recognized by commentators on the first general election in Spain for forty years. Spaniards, it was observed, must learn to play the 'game of democracy'.)

Turning activities into games adds to life another possible dimension of success and failure, winning or losing. It is a different dimension because one may simultaneously achieve one's purpose, but lose the game. Our huntsman for example, if he is very keen to return with the venison, may at the last moment abandon his bow and arrow or his rule about its being too easy to shoot close up and pick up his high-powered modern rifle and blast away. He has succeeded in his purpose, but lost the game. The general effect of a passion for gaming is to multiply occasions of winning and losing, of success and failure. And this effect is achieved by setting up closed systems within which winning and losing may be scored. A game of poker, chess or monopoly is a sealed system in principle independent of what goes on in the real world. Similarly, when purposive activities are, so to speak, 'gamed', we may correspondingly lose sight of what is, in technical terms, their real purpose. Those gallant English and French gentlemen at the battle of Fontenoy who each insisted that the troops of the other should fire first have often been regarded as lost to all reality (especially, no doubt, by their suffering troops), for the point of battles is to subdue the opponent, not to display one's gallantry. The French revolutionaries actually guillotined the general commanding the defence of Strasbourg who surrendered the town after the walls had been breached several times, honourable surrender under these circumstances being permitted by the then recognized rules of the game of war. This direly purposive note struck by the revolutionaries was the authentic tone of the coming era and exactly what Burke lamented in saying that the age of chivalry was dead.

While everyone is likely in one way or another to play games of various kinds, those whose lives are essentially subject to 'governors' in Sir Thomas Elyot's sense (to teachers, husbands, masters) cannot independently play what I have called the game of life. Women, children, servants, all those whose special situation has for one reason or another been essentially subordinate, generally play what we may call team games, and many arenas are closed to them. In competition between families, firms, states, churches and so on, they must play their part as supporters of their 'governor'.

In the middle ages as they are usually described, all society was united in a single functionally interdependent harmony which in principle (though doubtless not in practice) tended to inhibit the appearance of gaming, at least of individualistic gaming. The varying opinions of moralists about the passion of ambition has often been a comment upon individualistic gaming. In principle, the rulers protected and the governed served; in practice, merchants, nobles, prelates and kings played all sorts of games for all sorts of stakes. One way in which we may analyse the emergence of the modern world is in terms of the intensification of a disposition among more people than ever to construe life not in terms of a trial or a pilgrimage, nor in terms of filling one's station by doing one's duties, but as a game in which the point was to be a success at rising in the world.

Who, we may ask, would wish to resist this development? The obvious answer would seem to be the governors, and pre-eminently the governor of governors, namely, the sovereign power. For it will often be the case that the games of subordinates conflict with the games of the governors. It was in fact the case that the sovereigns of early modern Europe wanted to tax and control their subjects in pursuit of their own plans. Such plans were very commonly warlike, and the pursuance of these plans affected everything from technical education to the encouragement of production. There is the famous, possibly apocryphal, story of Louis xiv's minister, Colbert, calling together some of the merchants of Paris and asking how the authorities could help them, and after an embarrassed silence receiving the surly reply, 'Laissez-nous faire.' This is a good illustration of this kind of conflict of preoccupations and would make clear why governments had a preference for talking about duties, while subjects came to prefer talk about natural rights.

It is common to construe natural rights as essentially demands made by a particular class of people, demands which state the conditions of an expanding commercial activity. Natural rights, to give the view its crude but popular statement, was the ideology of the rising bourgeoisie. 'The real man', Marx tells us, 'is recognized only in the shape of the *egoistic* individual, the true man is recognized only in the shape of the *abstract citoyen*.'[30] Professor Macpherson sees in Hobbes and Locke the exponents of man as a limitless appropriator.[31] Nor is this view confined to Marxist writers. 'Civil society', Leo Strauss writes, 'merely creates the conditions under which the individuals can pursue their productive-acquisitive activity without obstruction.'[32] And he points out that 'in his thematic discussion of property, [Locke] is silent about any duties of charity'.[33]

Now on the actual behaviour of men in the seventeenth and eighteenth centuries much may be said, and much has been said. I do not know whether man was more of a wolf to man in those days than he was in times when the duty of charity was more noisily discussed. But

[30] Marx and Engels, *op. cit.*, p. 167.

[31] C. B. Macpherson, *The Political Theory of Possessive Individualism: Hobbes to Locke* (Oxford, 1962).

[32] L. Strauss, *op. cit.*, p. 246.

[33] *ibid.*, p. 248.

two things are immediately clear. The first is that the natural right to life, liberty and property does not *mean* that men ought ruthlessly to appropriate whatever property they can. For a variety of reasons, these men who, we are given to understand, were looking for a little philosophical perfume with which to conceal their rapacities, hit upon a doctrine of natural rights which led, within a generation or two, to the Clapham Sect and the abolition of the slave trade, the setting up of Sunday schools, the infestation of prisons with reformers, and a host of other activities arising from the growing eighteenth-century conviction that suffering was a bad thing. The logic of moral and political theories is a slow-burning fuse. It would be difficult to point to any evil that came into the world direct upon the heels of the doctrine of natural rights and easy to point to some that went out as a reasonably direct consequence of it. This seems to me to establish a *prima facie* case for doubting the assumption of these arguments, which is in any case without logical warrant, namely that the assertion of a particular moral belief, to wit in natural rights, involved a particular structure of motives, to wit egoism.

We need not doubt that much rapacity may be associated with the doctrine, but then much rapacity has been combined with all the great popular doctrines Europeans have ever entertained. What seems to me to have been less recognized is the significance of natural rights in opening up spaces within which people who felt themselves suffocated by the repetitive purposiveness of their lives might be allowed to play a part in the wider game of life. For one of the most obvious proposals for a variation in the rules of the game of life took the form of attempting to redefine who might be the individual players. Thus Mary Wollstonecraft writes of the way that women have been forced to live their lives within the purposiveness of procreation and childbearing, and adds in a footnote: 'A lively writer (I cannot recollect his name) asks what business women turned of forty have to do in the world.'[34] We have already seen the use of the idea of rights to make a space for children thought to be suffocated within the family union.

Natural rights doctrine is, then, a vindication of the space people need to play the game of life. The space is certainly affected by the legal, moral and technical rules that apply unavoidably to whatever we do in life. The natural right to worship God in one's own way (or in none) was prominent among the rights declared in eighteenth-century documents. This is in part a shift from a communal emphasis to an individual one, and it is no doubt partly a consequence of the growing currency of the view that God was a first mover rather than a perpetual providential meddler in the affairs of man. The kind of fear that made

[34] 'A Vindication of the Rights of Woman' in M. Wollstonecraft, *The Rights of Woman*, J. S. Mill, *The Subjection of Women*, Everyman's Library, (London, 1929, reprinted 1955), p. 7.

seventeenth-century Englishmen believe that fires and floods were expressions of God's displeasure at the community's tolerance of atheists like Hobbes seemed less plausible a century later and men could thus afford to indulge religious individualism. One aspect of the right claimed is that it permits each person to make his own particular version of the Pascalian wager with God. It is the innovative, the gambling, the playful use that a man—or a woman—could make of a right, that reveals the point of rights. If we take natural rights to be demands for substantial benefits rather than opportunities, we shall misunderstand their real character, just as Marx did. For Marx's remarks on natural rights as abstract exhibit him as someone incapable of comprehending the notion of life as a game. As he saw it, rights were demands, and the only way to understand the real character of these demands was to look to their actual outcome. That actual outcome was inevitably that, in each generation, some people did better than others, and hence, thinking always in purposive terms, Marx took the abstract character of natural rights as an ideological obfuscation (or mystification) of their real purpose. He believed that this purpose was revealed for all to see in their consequences, as devices for making the bourgeoisie rich and the proletariat poor. The real problem, it followed, was how to construct a society which could be managed in such a way that the consequences (that is satisfaction of need) of possessing rights could be provided for everyone. The gaming element of life disappears, and a productive purpose takes its place.

Marx was right, then, to suggest that natural rights separate man from man, but he was wrong to attribute the separating impulse entirely to something called 'egoism'. The impulse to assert rights derives, I suggest, from a set of considerations that operate in the thought of modern Europeans, and of all who have been influenced by them, which we may call gaming. Gaming requires such separation if it is to have, as we might say, 'free play'. But these are purely formal considerations, yielding formal rights. It is a complete misunderstanding of them to say, 'The Declaration of the Rights of Man was in effect a model charter of bourgeois society'[35] if by this is meant that natural rights expressed the demands of one determinate block of men against another determinate block of men. It is true that an inalienable right to life, liberty and the pursuit of happiness separates men in that it formally prohibits them from selling themselves into slavery. But it is otherwise compatible with virtually any form of union human beings may choose, from the communitarian settlements of nineteenth-century America to the kibbutzim of modern Israel. There is no logical connection between a right and any particular motive for exercising it; and leaving logic aside, the actual

[35] Alvin Gouldner, *The Dialectic of Ideology and Technology* (London and New York, 1976), p. 199.

exercise of natural rights has in fact been compatible with the full range of human thought and feeling.

IV Ideology versus gaming

I am arguing, then, that alongside the purposiveness in terms of which we often interpret activities (and sometimes think we exhaust them) there are to be found considerations of a gaming kind, and that an understanding of natural rights requires that we should take this element into account. But what then are we to make of the enormous variety of rights that the modern world has more recently brought forward? Sir Leslie Scarman,[36] in a lecture on human rights, spoke of the original natural rights as now somewhat ancient instruments and went on to say that great strides have been made by mankind generally in the identification of rights since 1948. The rights he was particularly thinking of were what he and the United Nations alike called social and economic rights. He was quite clear about the fact that such rights could only be guaranteed if money and a highly sophisticated administrative apparatus were available. And lumping together all these rights, he remarked that human rights were those rights which must be protected if the government were to be a rightful government. Similarly John Rawls, in discussing inequalities, talks of 'prestige or wealth, or liability to taxation and compulsory services'.[37] It is clear that things like wealth, and holidays with pay, and pension schemes, cannot be interpreted as 'proposals about rules of the game' as I have so far interpreted natural rights. And this brings me to some concluding remarks about ideology.

I shall simply have to stipulate what I mean by it. I take ideology to be any comprehensive diagnosis of the human condition which points toward a purification of society in terms of race, class, nation, or some similar sociological abstraction, as providing an ultimately better and non-political condition of things. Thus Marxism, which is the master ideology of our time, explains the modern world in terms of alienation and the crisis of capitalism, tells us how we got into our present predicament (the technical word is 'crisis') and looks forward to the withering away of the state, a condition in which the rights of man will be pointless because they would be irrelevant to the free flow of human spontaneity. The homogeneously racial or national states which have been adumbrated by other thinkers have been no more friendly to such devices as natural rights and liberal democracy. All such doctrines are uniformly hostile to what I have been calling governors, and the entire

[36] Sir Leslie Scarman, centenary celebration lecture in the University of London, 13 October 1976.

[37] J. Rawls, 'Justice as Fairness', *Philosophical Review* LXVII (1958), pp. 164–94 at p. 167.

function of government is usually dissolved into the arrangements of society itself. These arrangements are thought to be spontaneously maintained.

Now, given such a conception of human life, natural or 'separating' rights appear to be inappropriate because they are thought to presuppose the element of mistrust and hostility between human beings that Marx, as we saw, considered deplorable. It might be imagined that what I have called 'uniting' rights would still be appropriate, and it is indeed difficult to imagine human situations which could not plausibly be described in such terms. But the very word 'describing' here brings out clearly what would be at issue. In a fully articulated ideological world, human spontaneity does for itself (if I may parody Paine) everything that was hitherto done for it by the apparatus of prescription. When the state has withered away, men naturally behave in the cooperative manner which hitherto has been so inefficiently imposed by laws and the repressive apparatus of the state. Hence it seems likely that, while rights and duties might still be used to describe the details of human cooperation, their age-old prescriptive connotations would make them potentially unsuitable for the purpose. They would be unrealistic.

Nevertheless, although rights and ideology are in this sense fundamentally incompatible, the rhetorical climate of the present century has made it irresistible for those who have an ideological conception of human life both to use the term and to bend it closer to their own conceptions; hence the appearance of what are now called social and economic rights, things whose content is not some abstract *space* or liberty, but rather a specific sort of *thing*—pensions in old age, for example, or holidays with pay. The transition involved here may be illustrated by an expression like 'the right to work' which, in its earlier use as one among a variety of natural rights, stated a rule by which the willing and able should not be prevented from working on irrelevant grounds, but which as a social right amounts to the demand that an actual job should actually be provided.

The fulfilment of rights like this, as Scarman made clear, requires not only specific legal and political arrangements, but also money. Such rights are thus much more dependent upon circumstances than the rights we have been discussing in this chapter. They do not relate to rules in the same way as natural rights, and it is entirely plausible to see them as *demands* for specific things. They cannot for a moment be seen as having anything to do with the gaming element we have found in traditional natural rights; indeed they are incomprehensible unless we recognize a switch away from the conception of life as a kind of game to one of human life as the production and consumption of satisfactions. Social and economic rights are claims to a share of the productive totality of a community construed as if it were a factory;

and indeed part of the point of such claims is the demand that society should actually become a factory.

It follows from what I have been arguing that there are at least two significant discontinuities in the history of rights. The first of these is the discontinuity between natural law and natural rights. Natural rights are entirely different things from natural law. They operate in a largely different sphere and are used for different purposes. The second of these discontinuities is the switch from a political to an ideological notion of rights, usually marked by a change in the partnering words that are a constant feature of the way in which the term 'rights' is used. Political and civil rights, as they are now discussed, are the legitimate descendants of natural rights and are ways of discussing liberty and proposing a rule of the game, in terms of which it is the frustrator rather than the initiator of an action on whom the onus of justification lies. Social and economic rights usually involve a conception of society as a productive system, and constitute demands about the allocation of what is produced. (Even here, however, it is misleading to construe such rights *merely* as demands. A crucial element has been left out. It is best captured in some remarks by Alexis de Tocqueville in his *Memoir on Pauperism*:

> There is nothing which, generally speaking, elevates and sustains the human spirit more than the idea of rights. There is something great and virile in the idea of right which removes from any request its suppliant character, and places the one who claims it on the same level as the one who grants it. But the right of the poor to obtain society's help is unique in that instead of elevating the heart of the man who exercises it, it lowers him.[38]

And just as we may misunderstand natural law by projecting it back on what is involved in natural rights, so we shall misunderstand natural rights if we project back upon it the features of social and economic rights. Natural rights are not demands; they are proposals about changing rules and *this*, of course, may be demanded. But the demanding is contingent to the character of a right.

If this argument is correct, the mistake that has usually been made about the character of natural rights is similar to that made by the possibly apocryphal maharajah of earlier days who, observing Englishmen sweating and grunting under the hot sun as they played cricket, wondered why they did not get their servants to do it for them. Life conceived as a game also produces much sweating and grunting, but it brings its own reward to some. Ideology, however, amounts to the proposal to send games back to the nursery and expel them from

[38] A. de Tocqueville and G. de Beaumont, *Tocqueville and Beaumont on Social Reform*, edited and translated by S. Drescher (New York and London, 1968), p. 17.

the serious work of life. And modern politics is in part a continuing meditation on how these two human propensities—that which sees life as a game, and that which wishes to enforce a strict split between the purposive and the gaming—may accommodate each other.

3

Human rights, legal rights and social change

John Kleinig

In 1822 Jefferson wrote that 'nothing . . . is unchangeable but the inherent and unalienable rights of man.'[1] With the benefit of hindsight Jefferson's claim appears, if not wrong, at least oversimplified. Jefferson was too deeply immersed in the controversies and presuppositions of his time to see the extent to which the classic declarations of the eighteenth century reflected a prevailing set of circumstances and values. The continuity that can be traced between those declarations and contemporary statements may reflect no more than a continuity in the social structures prevailing then and now in the Western world. But there have also been significant shifts in content and emphasis which cannot be ignored. To close one's eyes to these changes may be to invest the classic rights with an illegitimate authority, a givenness which impedes rather than facilitates moral understanding and practice.

The changes that have occurred are of various kinds:

1 Perhaps the most obvious shift has been from the starkly protective rights of the eighteenth-century declarations to the strong welfare orientation found in contemporary documents. Articles 22–27 of the United Nations Declaration of Human Rights (1948) would have been quite out of keeping with the purposes of the Virginia Declaration of Rights (1776), the Declaration of Independence of the United States (1776), the Declaration of the Rights of Man and of Citizens (1789). For the overriding concern of these latter was to establish a *distance* from oppressive structures and regimes which would enable human flourishing to take place. Further, these structures and regimes were conceived politically rather than socially, and the applicability of the declarations to women and slaves remained a moot point.

It is not only in the additions that this shift can be observed. The so-called 'great rights' have also undergone a metamorphosis. In

[1] Quoted in Richard Hofstadter, *The American Political Tradition and the Men Who Made It* (New York, 1948, reprinted in paperback 1954), p. 44.

Blackstone, the right to life was subsumed under 'the right of personal security', and consisted in 'a person's legal and uninterrupted enjoyment of his life, his limbs, his body, his health, and his reputation'.[2] Under current interpretations, that protection has been extended to cover psychological suffering and apprehension of injury, offensive noises and odours, and invasions of privacy. Moreover, it is now frequently interpreted to include various state-guaranteed contributions designed to provide in a positive way for 'enjoyment' of life. The focus has shifted from quantity to quality of life. Work, opportunity for leisure, food, shelter, clothing and health care are all clustered round contemporary accounts of the right to life.[3] This expansion in the scope of the right to life (and the increase in welfare rights generally) has been accompanied by change in the scope and emphasis of the right to liberty. As other rights have increased in scope, the right to non-interference has contracted and there has developed in its place a more positive understanding—liberty as autonomy or self-government.[4]

2   Although human rights documents are now, as in the eighteenth century, political documents, and thus focus on the role of government in the maintenance of rights,[5] they nevertheless reflect a recognition of a broader range of threats from a greater variety of sources than early documents. The growth of industrialization and supertechnologies, the development of multinational corporations and capitalist ownership, the increased sense of internationalism and global contraction ('the global village'), have forced an awareness of aspects of human rights which had previously been overlooked or not been thought to need spelling out. Most of the classic documents include the right to property, and this has played an important ideological role in the development of Western-style democracies.[6] But in one of the most recent documents, the International Covenant on Economic, Social and Cultural Rights (1966), the right to own property is not explicitly reaffirmed (contrast the United Nations Declaration of 1948). On the other hand, a pre-eminent position has been given to the

---

[2] Sir William Blackstone, *Commentaries on the Laws of England* (4 vols, Oxford, 1765–9) I, p. 129.

[3] See Hugo Bedau, 'The Right to Life', *Monist* LII (1968), pp. 550–72; Joel Feinberg, *Social Philosophy* (Englewood Cliffs, N.J., 1973), pp. 61, 70–71.

[4] See D. G. Ritchie's trenchant criticism of Herbert Spencer in *Natural Rights* (London, 1894), p. 139. In his recent book, *Taking Rights Seriously* (London, 1977), chapter 12, Ronald Dworkin suggests that the traditional right to liberty should be abandoned in favour of the right to (certain) liberties.

[5] The reason no doubt being the continuing belief in government as the legitimized source of coercive power in society.

[6] Largely through Jefferson's influence, the right to property was not included in the Declaration of Independence of the United States. This was not, however, because he was opposed to private property, but because he saw it as a civil rather than a natural right.

right of national self-determination. As political documents, these statements are, of course, liable to variations in interpretation, but it can hardly be denied that they evidence both the historical character of the eighteenth-century declarations and the somewhat changed circumstances and appreciations of the latter part of the twentieth century.

3   One further change of a more theoretical nature deserves to be noted. Those writers of the seventeenth and eighteenth centuries who popularized the vocabulary of human rights succeeded largely because of the common acceptance of natural law. Within its ethos, talk of (natural) rights constituted a natural and desirable extension to socio-moral vocabulary. This of course was not the only reason for speaking specifically of 'rights': their primary association with politico-legal power was peculiarly suited to their politico-moral purpose. Nevertheless, the introduction of rights-talk into moral discourse was made much easier by the dominance of natural law theory. Since then, in the Anglo-American tradition, natural law has suffered something of a decline (at least its contemporary defenders are put on the defensive).[7] Yet talk of human (and moral) rights has burgeoned, not diminished. And it has continued, for the most part, with all the seriousness of yore. Some years ago E. F. Carritt argued that 'the disrepute into which natural rights fell was due to the temerity of those who presumed to define and catalogue them as inalienable in declarations of independence and constitutional preambles.'[8] But while it is true that the seventeenth-century characterizations of rights as 'natural, imprescriptible and inalienable' attracted a good deal of criticism (particularly from Bentham, Ritchie and others in the utilitarian tradition), this did not deter the framers of the constitution of the French Fourth Republic (1946; reaffirmed in 1958) and of the International Covenant on Economic, Social and Cultural Rights (1966) from continuing to speak of their inalienability.

Nevertheless, the fact that human rights-talk has been cut free from its moorings in natural law vocabulary leads us to pose the serious question whether it is now a ship adrift on the sea of political rhetoric, at the mercy of this or that ideological wind, or whether it may still possess a significant moral as well as political function. In what relation does it stand to the traditional vocabulary of ethics? Does it have a distinctive logic of its own, or can it be analysed without remainder into 'the language of obligation'?[9] In relation to these questions it is now commonly argued that there is a distinct vocabulary of rights, to

---

[7] The influence of utilitarianism has been largely responsible for this. Rights-talk has never fitted comfortably into utilitarian theory.

[8] E. F. Carritt, *Ethical and Political Thinking* (Oxford 1947), pp. 78–9.

[9] I am using the phrase 'the language of obligation' simply as a device for referring to traditional ethical vocabulary.

be explicated by reference to the vocabulary of legal rights, and not reducible to 'the language of obligation'. It is my purpose to criticize this view, and to offer an alternative account of human rights which recognizes their distinctiveness without departing from 'the language of obligation'.

I have already observed that the vocabulary of rights was introduced into a moral discourse for which it had been prepared by the natural law tradition. It would be going too far to suggest that this would not have occurred but for that tradition, since legal models for moral discourse have not been exclusive to natural law theory. Nevertheless the historical roots of moral rights discourse should not be forgotten. Nor should we forget that the values which rights-talk was designed to assert and secure did not suddenly emerge into moral consciousness for the first time in the seventeenth century, even though they constituted a reaction against socio-political arrangements which had ignored or abrogated them. There has always existed a moral tradition emphasizing 'the inherent dignity of the human person'.[10] Thus, when Joel Feinberg argues that 'a world without claim-rights, no matter how full of benevolence and devotion to duty, would suffer an immense moral impoverishment', since it would fail to be a world 'in which all persons, as actual or potential claimants, are dignified objects of respect, both in their own eyes and in the view of others',[11] we must take him to be talking about the concept of a right and not about the terminology of rights. In the seventeenth century, recognition of the proper claims of individuals on the consideration of others found its expression in the vocabulary of rights. Even though, in line with the prevailing mood, this was not accorded the universality it now is (though there are reasons for doubting that, for many in contemporary society, talk of 'human' rights is anything more than a form of words), the singling out of certain features of the moral landscape as rights served to highlight them in a politically useful way.

In making these observations, I do not want to cast a shadow over the vocabulary of rights. In many ways, the use of rights-talk to safeguard human dignity is particularly happy. It does not have the disadvantages of neologism; the legal territory from which it comes is well trodden, facilitating the task of explication; the coercive possibilities of legal rights have provided political muscle for moral rights-talk; and the personal advantage or benefit generally implicit in legal rights-talk is helpful in drawing attention to the value of moral and human rights. Nevertheless, if we lose sight of the circumstances surrounding its introduction, we run the risk of it getting out of hand.

[10] From the preamble to the International Covenant on Economic, Social and Cultural Rights (1966).

[11] Feinberg, *op. cit.*, pp. 58, 59; see also his 'The Nature and Value of Rights', *Journal of Value Inquiry* IV (1970), pp. 243–57.

Certain botanical and zoological analogies are apposite: some plant and animal species which have been introduced to a country in order to deal with natural deficiencies or pests have flourished so well in the new environment that they have themselves eventually become pests. That possibility exists with conceptual imports as well. In the case of rights-talk, which has more and more become the standard moral currency, the medium of moral exchange, this possibility has I think been actualized and we have seen a gradual edging out of other important dimensions of our moral transactions.[12] I think this is evidenced by the following commonplaces in contemporary discussions of rights—1) the conception of rights as discretionary powers; 2) the heavily jurisprudential analyses of human rights; and 3) the kind of priority given to human rights in moral reasoning. In what follows I propose to approach my own position by way of a critique of these commonplaces.

I

Let us go back, briefly, to Locke. In his view, all men are 'the workmanship of one omnipotent, and infinitely wise Maker; all the servants of one sovereign Master, sent into the world by His order, and about His business'.[13] The boundaries of men's service are given by the law of nature, but within those boundaries they have 'perfect freedom to order their actions, and dispose of their possessions . . . as they think fit . . . without asking leave, or depending upon the will of any other man'.[14] There is thus, behind Locke's picture of men in a state of nature, a vision of what human existence might be, and it is the conditions of its realization which constitute the rationale for men's rights. Without such rights their lives and service must remain impoverished and unfulfilled. For Locke, as indeed for others of his time, rights did not constitute spheres of autonomy bounded *only* by the rights of others. They were circumscribed by the law of nature, as well as by the rights of others. The right to life gave men no right to dispose of their own lives. What was central to rights was the moral constraint that they constituted on the behaviour of others, generally to forbear, but occasionally also to provide.[15]

Lockian rights allow of only limited discretion, and in this they differ from a standard account of legal rights, according to which they

---

[12] The degeneration of rights-talk into mere political sloganeering is well illustrated by Nan Berger's *Rights: a Handbook for People under Age* (Harmondsworth, 1974) and in assertions of the 'right to a tobacco-free job', the 'right to sunshine', the 'right of a father to be present in the delivery room', the 'right to a sex break' cited in the *Hastings Center Report* VII (1977), p. 4.

[13] John Locke, *Second Treatise of Civil Government*, chapter 2, §6.

[14] *ibid.*, §4.

[15] Locke, *First Treatise of Civil Government*, chapter 4, §42.

are thought of as centrally and essentially discretionary. While it would be mistaken to ignore the close connection between rights and freedom, a connection which Locke himself acknowledges, his view is better understood in terms of advantage than of discretionary power.

It can of course be questioned whether the standard account of legal rights as discretionary powers is correct. I do not myself find it completely convincing: the legal right to an education seems to be also a legal duty; and as well as the right to vote there is, in some countries at least, also a legal duty to vote. Those committed to a discretionary view of rights generally argue that in these circumstances there are no rights, only duties. But if rights are seen primarily as advantages, that conclusion is not necessary.

This difficulty aside, what is to be said for the discretionary view? Most influential has been Professor H. L. A. Hart, who argues that it is being morally in a position to determine by one's choice how another will act, and in this way to limit the other's freedom of choice, that makes it appropriate to speak of a person's having a right, not the fact that he stands to benefit. Consequently, 'if common usage sanctions talk of the rights of animals or babies it makes an idle use of the expression "a right", which will confuse the situation with other different moral situations where the expression "a right" has a specific force and cannot be replaced by other moral expressions.'[16] Being a right-holder presupposes capacities for choice not possessed by animals and babies. More specifically, S. I. Benn argues that to be a right-holder a being must possess the sort of interests which organize and give consistent direction to otherwise diverse activity. For only of such is the kind of claiming or waiving power distinctive of rights possible. For this reason, Benn does not think that attempts to relocate the power to claim in some proxy do full justice to the idea of a right. For 'the discretionary power of someone appointed as trustee or guardian *ad litem* would be constrained by the condition that the power be exercised only for the advantage of the beneficiary.' A right-holder, however, may exercise his rights for his disadvantage as well as his advantage. His rights are not necessarily linked to his welfare interests, but instead to 'the kind of interests that give a consistent direction to his activities; they are normative resources that enable him, by controlling the actions of others, to manipulate his social environment for his own ends—*whatever* those ends may be.'[17]

---

[16] H. L. A. Hart, 'Are there any Natural Rights?', *Philosophical Review* LXIV (1955), pp. 175–91 at p. 181.
[17] S. I. Benn, 'Personal Freedom and Environmental Ethics: the Moral Inequality of Species', a paper presented to the World Congress of the International Association for Philosophy of Law and Social Philosophy, St Louis, 1975, and published in *Equality and Freedom: International and Comparative Jurisprudence*, edited by G. Dorsey (3 vols, New York and Leiden, 1977) II, pp. 401–24, at p. 407.

According to the discretionary view, if *A* has a right to *x* against *B*, then *B*'s duty to *A* rests on *A*'s exercising his right. *A*'s right is simply his being in a position to require the forbearance or contribution of another. Hart puts it thus: 'The precise figure is not that of two persons bound by a chain, but of *one* person bound, the other end of the chain lying in the hands of another to use if he chooses.'[18] There is an ambiguity in Hart's figure which is symptomatic of an underlying confusion in the discretionary position. It is not clear whether in the latter figure *B* is simply bound, or bound *to A*. The context suggests that Hart wants to say that *B* is bound to *A*. Yet the picture of the chain simply 'lying' in *A*'s hand to be used only 'if he chooses' suggests that *B* is not bound to *A unless A* grips the chain. Put more schematically, the statement form '*A* has a right to *x* against *B*' may be thought to entail either '*B* has a duty to give *x* to *A* unless *A* chooses otherwise' or '*B* has a duty to give *x* to *A* only if *A* chooses.' It may be questioned whether either of these is entailed (contented slaves still have their rights violated); but if we are to choose that which most nearly approximates to the discretionary element in rights-talk, the first formulation seems more accurate. Your duty to respect my rights does not have to wait for my assertion of them, and if I waive them I release you from what is *already* due me. Thus, if I have a right against you, the chain which binds you does not merely *lie* in my hand. I have a firm grip on it, though I may release it. However, advocates of the discretionary position tend to adopt the second formulation, and this explains their exclusion of babies and animals from the company of right-holders. For the second, though not the first, formulation presupposes the right-holder's actual ability to choose. There is no reason, therefore, why the discretionary aspect of rights-talk needs to be tied directly to the interests possessed by actual choosers rather than the welfare interests of beings capable of benefiting in themselves and who are at best potential choosers.[19]

Against the view that rights are advantages, Hart argues that cases may be found where the right-holder does not benefit from its exercise—not because of some unexpected intervention, but because the beneficiary is a third party.[20] Thus if *B* promises *A* in return for some favour that he will look after *A*'s aged mother, *A* has a right against *B*, though it is not *A*, but *A*'s mother, who benefits. Hart's view has not gone unchallenged.[21] However, if he is right about this case it

[18] Hart, *op. cit.*, p. 181.

[19] Being a chooser is a condition for the possession of certain rights (for example to vote), but not all rights. If we do not wish to ascribe rights to animals it is not, I believe, because they are not actual or potential choosers, but because we do not consider their welfare interests important enough to justify securing them by force.

[20] *ibid.*, p. 180.

[21] For example, David Lyons, 'Rights, Claimants, and Beneficiaries', *American Philosophical Quarterly* VI (1969), pp. 173–85.

constitutes one of only a narrow class of cases in which the beneficiary is not the right-holder, and is more appropriately viewed as flowing from the character of promises, contracts and agreements than as showing the inadequacy of the beneficiary theory.[22] But I am not convinced that Hart is right about the case, and would suggest that its plausibility arises from a too narrow conception of advantage as benefit. In the case under consideration A's mother will certainly benefit if B keeps his promise. But this does not show that A is not also advantaged; quite the contrary. A's advantage will reside in the securing of his interest (stake) in his mother's welfare. Were A to have no interest at all in his mother's welfare, B's promise to him would be pointless as would be the ascription of a right to A.

I would suggest, then, that significant difficulties attach to the view of rights as necessarily discretionary powers, and that objections to the main alternative are not persuasive. To some extent the view that human and moral rights are discretionary powers is a carry over from legal rights, or at least a certain common view of legal rights, though even legal rights do not always allow for waiver (for example, the rejection of consent as a defence in certain criminal cases, as well as the examples previously cited). This, I believe, has come about as a result of the identification of rights-talk with the influential individualistic and libertarian traditions in Anglo-American culture, with their essentially negative conception of liberty. Although Locke's doctrine of rights has often been seen as the foundation for that tradition, and there is undoubtedly some truth in that, nevertheless I believe his position was rather more narrowly circumscribed than is commonly believed.[23]

II

As might be expected from earlier remarks, I am not persuaded by Professor Wellman's 'new conception of human rights', set out below. It seems to me to be an attempt to increase the exactness of the analogy between legal and human rights without regard to the point of human rights-talk. Let me attempt to spell this out.

First of all, Wellman is quite right to see in human rights-talk a pervasive vagueness. The rights to life and privacy are not rights to narrowly defined behaviour on the part of others, but comprise a complex of claims for which 'life' and 'privacy' are but categorial names. As a step towards overcoming this indefiniteness, Wellman proposes to introduce into the discussion a set of legal distinctions first

---

[22] Hart's use of 'special' rights to explicate rights in general imports into his account non-general characteristics.

[23] See, for example, Virginia Held, 'John Locke on Robert Nozick', *Social Research* XLIII (1976), pp. 171–95.

mapped out in detail by Wesley Hohfeld. Hohfeld showed that in legal discussion lawyers had tended to use the term 'a right' to refer indiscriminately to a number of distinct jural relations—what he called claims, liberties, powers and immunities. Wellman seems to suggest that legal rights, on the Hohfeldian model, constitute a cluster of claims, liberties, powers and immunities unified by a core advantage. I doubt whether Hohfeld saw the matter that way, but that is not my concern here. My reservations are directed towards Professor Wellman's use of these distinctions in explicating human rights.

To bring this out, I need to draw attention to an important feature of rights, both legal and moral, and this is their connection with coercive power. Early declarations of rights were regarded as justifications for revolution and other acts of political violence. Bentham saw in the appeal to natural rights the use of 'terrorist language'.[24] And Professor Hart also sees in relation to rights 'a special congruity in the use of force or the threat of force'. The point is not that right-holders *actually* possess the power to coerce others but that the use of force or the threat of force to secure compliance with the behaviour comprehended by the right would be appropriate. This, I believe, constitutes the justification for introducing rights-talk into the moral domain. Rights mark out moral considerations of such importance that the use of force to guarantee them would normally be justifiable. This 'special congruity' in the use or threat of force is supported by the usual account of rights as having correlative duties (claim-rights in Hohfeldian terminology), but is obscured in Wellman's account. Whatever confusions may have plagued the legal discussion of rights, it is fairly clear that those who borrowed the vocabulary of rights from legal discourse had in mind rights *stricto sensu*, and not liberties, powers, and immunities. I do not mean to suggest that there are not implied in human rights certain 'liberties', 'powers' and 'immunities', as well as claims, though I think the legal language distracting and unnecessary. The point is rather that these other relations are only secondary. This seems to me to be well illustrated by Wellman's discussion of the right to privacy, where the weight falls on certain core claims, and not on other associated liberties and so on.

In assuming human rights-talk to be unproblematic, needing only the kinds of refinement suggested by Hohfeld's schema, Wellman overlooks the fundamental problem raised by the importation of rights-talk into moral discourse. The first question to be asked is not: 'Can we give this terminology greater precision?' but 'For what purpose was this terminology employed?' That second question, I would suggest, is to be answered as follows: human rights represent those minimum conditions under which human beings can flourish

---

[24] Jeremy Bentham, selections from *Anarchical Fallacies*, as reprinted in A. I. Melden, editor, *Human Rights* (Belmont, California, 1970), pp. 28–39, at p. 32.

(that is as moral agents) and which ought to be secured for them, if necessary by force. The close connection between rights and the justifiable employment of coercion arises from the importance of the interests they are designed to secure, namely the welfare interests of individuals. Welfare interests are *minima*, those more or less indispensable preconditions for the pursuit and fulfilment of characteristically human interests, and which constitute human life an object of dignity and respect.[25] This unambiguous insistence that there are some interests of such importance that their coercive protection or securing is justified is muted by Wellman's attempt to see these interests as clusters of claims, liberties, powers and immunities, unified by some core advantage.

It does not seem to me that the problem with human rights-talk lies in ambiguity concerning its modality or modalities, but with the content of those basic interests which it seeks to highlight. For at the back of rights-talk there lies a conception of human existence for which there are minimum requirements, and though welfare interests tend to be fairly neutral as between competing 'visions' of human life, they are not sufficiently neutral to obviate all controversy. This, I take it, lies behind the differences between libertarian and socialist catalogues of human rights, and constitutes the most intractable dispute in this area.

The idea of human rights as minimum conditions for human flourishing helps to explain the emergence of the right to privacy. It is a right which finds no explicit formulation in the early documents on human rights, despite its strongly protective overtones. That it has now received explicit formulation is in large measure due to changes in our historical circumstances—particularly in the technology available to governments and other organizations—and, consequently, in our awareness of things which constitute some threat to our development as persons with 'inherent dignity'. Privacy, best thought of, I believe, in terms of the control one has over what is known concerning oneself, insofar as this bears on one's conception of oneself as a moral agent, has come to be threatened by a range of devices more extensive and subtle than ever before, thus justifying a redrafting of our catalogue of rights to make quite explicit what previously was either submerged in one of the traditional rights or not seen to require protection.

We do human rights-talk an injustice, I believe, by endeavouring to develop a logic of it to parallel legal rights discourse. Though the introduction of rights-talk into the vocabulary of socio-moral discourse was no accident, its role is the role it had for the writers of the seventeenth and eighteenth centuries, where legal rights were conceived of as enforceable advantages. The introduction of rights-

[25] I have treated the idea of a welfare interest in greater detail in 'Crime and the Concept of Harm', *American Philosophical Quarterly* XIV (1978), pp. 27–36.

talk into moral vocabulary did not herald a radical new moral discovery, but emphasized certain long acknowledged moral requirements that had been ignored by the sources of coercive power in society.

III

There is a further consequence of the expansion of legal rights vocabulary into the moral realm which concerns me. This is the current tendency to accord rights an exaggerated role in the moral life. There has been a noticeable tendency in recent moral discussion to frame issues as far as possible in terms of rights.[26] This is particularly evident in liberationist literature, in which the demand for recognition on the part of women, children, blacks and minority groups has frequently concentrated on rights. Insofar as rights constitute the minimum requirements for personhood, the importance of securing them is not to be gainsaid. But there is much more to adequate moral relationships than the bare recognition of rights, and this is frequently forgotten in the course of campaigning. Unless there is love, care and concern for others as individuals, *in addition to* the recognition of rights, there remains a moral lack in interpersonal relationships. There is something morally inadequate in doing something for another because it is the other's due. Actions motivated simply by the rights of others remain anonymous or impersonal, whereas if motivated by love, care or concern for the other their focus is on the other's particularity. Only relations of the latter kind are morally adequate. They are person-specific, whereas rights are 'species'-specific.

Again, this is not intended to underrate the importance of rights as socio-moral requirements. But I think it suggests that rights-talk, if it is not to be abused, must be seen in a wider moral context and not permitted to get out of hand. The wider context is one in which the primary moral relations of love, care and concern have broken down, and we need to fall back onto the auxiliary apparatus of rights. Where people do love and care for each other, there is no need for recourse to rights-*talk*, since what is due to the other will be encompassed within the loving or caring relationship.[27] But when love and care no longer exist or have been distorted as in bureaucratic or class-based societies, then the language of rights must be appealed to in order to maintain or recover the minima of interpersonal morality.

[26] See note 12 above.

[27] What I mean here is that love and care must have regard to the *kind* of thing that is their object, as well as its particularity. In the case of love and care for another person, it will involve an acknowledgement of the other's welfare interests, including the other's welfare interest in freedom. Where love and care stifle, as Benn suggests they might, they are defective *as* love and care.

IV

Our language is not to be conceived of on the model of an arbitrarily taken photograph, an aimless and passive representation of the world 'out there'. Rather, it reflects a deliberate ordering of that world, including human behaviour in all its aspects, according to shared interests. Some of these shared interests have become points of concentrated focus, and there have developed round them clusters of interconnected concepts which together form what might be called 'spheres of discourse'. Concepts formed within those spheres generally need to be explicated by reference to other concepts drawn from the same sphere, though the sphere itself can be understood by reference to more generally shared interests. Thus the term 'bail', formed from within the legal sphere of discourse, requires explication in terms of other legal concepts, the term 'electron', formed from within the discourse of the physical sciences, requires explication in terms of other scientific concepts, and the term 'lie' formed from within the moral sphere of discourse, is to be explicated by reference to other moral notions. This of course is highly schematic, and should not be taken to imply lack of change or even complete consistency within those spheres or even any rigid separation between them, any more than human interests are rigidly separated. Nevertheless, since there are different standpoints or emphases from which we want to consider the world, a world which moreover possesses its own diversity, it might be anticipated that attempts to reduce language to a unitary conceptual schema (such as was attempted by the logical atomists) will fail.

Within the foregoing framework, rights are legal concepts, to be explicated primarily by reference to other legal concepts. Herein lies the contribution of Hohfeld and those who have filled out his position. To transplant this terminology from the legal to the moral sphere of discourse is a major operation fraught with possibilities for confusion.[28] The political-coercive associations of rights-talk in its legal home constitute its distinctive contribution to moral discourse, where it marks out those advantages which are so fundamental to the pursuit of a worthwhile human life, that force may be enlisted in their service. We should not obscure this distinctive value by importing more of the legal associations than the world of moral discourse can properly and profitably accommodate.

---

[28] Apart from a number of instances where this has occurred in the development of institutionalized legal procedures, the problems have been well demonstrated in the social sciences where old vocabulary is taken over without careful thought, causing endless confusion.

4

A new conception of human rights

Carl Wellman

The demand that individual privacy be respected is becoming more common and more insistent in our age. This probably reflects a rapidly increasing need for privacy arising from converging ecological, cultural, technical and social changes. The population explosion together with modern urbanization have made it much more difficult for the individual to get away, physically and psychologically, from the crowd of strangers around him. The growing allegiance to political individualism and moral autonomy have caused the individual to resent and resist legal regulation and social interference more intensely. At a time when bugging and other techniques of surveillance have been perfected to an alarming degree, the development of computers enables us to store and retrieve vastly increased amounts of information about any specified individual in even very large populations. Finally, as organizations have grown larger in size and more bureaucratic in structure, their tendency to invade the life of the individual has grown apace.

In the United States, whatever may be the case in other societies, the legal system has responded to these changes by relying more and more heavily upon the constitutional right to privacy. Only recently has the student's right to privacy been protected by legal restrictions upon the kinds of information that may be put into his academic file, the length of time potentially adverse material may be kept in his file, and the conditions under which it may be released without his written consent. The bugging of one's premises or telephone is now recognized as a violation of the prohibition in the Fourth Amendment against unreasonable searches and seizures. And in the landmark decision of *Roe* v. *Wade* (410 US 113), the Supreme Court found state laws prohibiting abortion during the first six months of pregnancy a violation of the pregnant woman's constitutional right to privacy.

Since the constitution does not explicitly mention any right to privacy, one may wonder why the Supreme Court has repeatedly recognized it as a fundamental legal right. In the earlier case of *Griswold* v. *Connecticut* (381 US 479), it had been successfully argued that the right to privacy is one of the unenumerated rights retained by the people and guaranteed to them by the Ninth Amendment. Since these rights are said to be 'retained by' the people, they are taken to be rights prior to and independent of the constitution and to any laws made pursuant thereto. In short, the legal right to privacy is legally and morally grounded in the human right to privacy.

Unfortunately, any such appeal to human rights, whether made within a legal system or in the arena of political debate, raises at least three awkward philosophical questions. First, how do we know that there really is any human right to privacy? It is not just that there is widespread disagreement about the assertion, 'there is a human right to privacy'; philosophers and jurists have not given us any convincing account of the kind of evidence that could establish rationally the truth or falsehood of this statement. Second, assuming that there is a human right to privacy, what duties or obligations does it imply? It might imply that the state ought to establish and enforce a legal right to privacy or merely that it ought to refrain from invading the privacy of those subject to its jurisdiction. It might or might not imply that one state has an obligation to put economic or political pressure upon another state to cause that state to respect the privacy of the citizens of that second state. The legal philosopher has provided no helpful principles or method for determining just what the practical implications of any human right are. Third, precisely how is the content of the human right to privacy to be defined? Not only is the concept of privacy obscure and unexplained, it is far from clear what it means to say that someone has a *right to* privacy. Does this mean that second parties ought not to invade one's privacy or that it is never wrong to resist such invasions or both or neither of these things?

In this chapter, I propose to focus my attention on the third problem: how is the content of the human right to privacy to be defined? What concerns me is not so much the correct definition of this particular human right as the understanding of the way in which the content of any human right may best be conceived. For only if we can achieve a clear conception of the content of any specified human right can we fully understand what it means to assert or deny the existence of that right. And understanding what assertions of human rights mean is an essential preliminary to understanding what sort of evidence is required to establish their truth and what they logically imply.

The problem of defining the precise content of a mentioned right occurs in the law much as it does in the appeal to human rights. Just as we speak glibly of the human rights to privacy, security of person and an adequate standard of living, so we speak of the legal rights to life, free speech, and the equal protection of the laws. How, then, does the practising lawyer or presiding judge know precisely what in every detail is meant by such mere names and catch phrases? Often he does not; that is what lawsuits are all about. Nevertheless, this problem is much less serious in the law than in the sphere of human rights. Why?

The law provides two reasonably effective solutions to this problem of defining the content of any legal right, one practical and the other theoretical. Legal rights are institutional; they are created, defined and maintained by the legal system in some society. Hence, whenever their content proves to be insufficiently defined to cope with some new situation or case, they can be *re*defined by the legal institutions, particularly the legislature and the courts, that originally created them and continue to sustain them. Thus through a growing body of statutes and precedents, legal rights gradually achieve a precision and specificity sadly lacking in human rights. This sort of practical solution is not possible in the case of human rights. Since these rights, if they exist at all, exist prior to and independently of society and its institutions, they cannot be rendered determinate by the vote of any philosophical congress or the definition of any jurist. Fortunately, jurisprudence also offers a more theoretical solution to this problem. Wesley Hohfeld has identified certain legal conceptions that can be used to define, precisely and unambiguously, the content of any legal right.

Hohfeld identified and illustrated, but refused to define, eight fundamental legal conceptions—four conceptions of legal advantages and four of legal disadvantages. Since possessing a legal right is obviously having some sort of advantage in the law, it is the first four that primarily concern us here. Let us review them briefly. Our review is at one and the same time an articulation of four legal concepts and a characterization of four legal realities. They are:

1   *A legal liberty.* One party x has a legal liberty in face of some second party y to perform some action A if and only if x has no legal duty to y to refrain from doing A. I have, for example, the legal liberty in face of Professor Tay to use her name in this example; I do not, however, have the legal liberty of referring to her in any libellous manner. Let us suppose that I have secretly, and profitably, contracted with Professor Kamenka to mention him rather than Professor Tay at this point. I would still have the legal liberty in face of Professor Tay to use her name here, for I have no legal duty *to her* to refrain from doing so. But I would not have the legal liberty vis-à-vis Professor Kamenka to mention Professor Tay here, for under our contract I have a legal duty to him not to do so.

2   *A legal claim.* One party x has a legal claim against some second party y that y do some action A if and only if y has a legal duty to x to do A. Thus, I have a legal claim against Jones, to whom I loaned ten dollars on the understanding that he repay me today, that he repay me

today; similarly, I have a legal claim against Smith, whoever Smith may be, that he not strike me.

3   *A legal power.* One party x has a legal power over some second party y to bring about some specific legal consequence C for y if and only if some voluntary action of x would be legally recognized as having this consequence for y. For example, a policeman has the legal power over a fleeing suspect to place him under arrest, and the owner of a car has the legal power over someone offering to buy his car of making him the new owner of the car.

4   *A legal immunity.* One party x has a legal immunity against some second party y from some specified legal consequence C if and only if y lacks the legal power to do any action whatsoever that would be recognized by the law as having the consequence C for x. Thus, I have a legal immunity against my wife's renouncing my United Sates citizenship, but I lack a legal immunity against her spending the monies in our joint bank account. These, roughly indicated and briefly illustrated, are the four legal advantages Hohfeld takes to be fundamental in the law.[1] (The four corresponding legal disadvantages are a legal no-claim, a legal duty, a legal liability and a legal disability.)

Hohfeld shows us in quotation after quotation how the expression 'a right' is used almost indiscriminately to refer to any one of these four legal advantages. No one who has studied Hohfeld can imagine for a moment that the content of the right to life is simply life. He forces us to ask whether the right to life is essentially the liberty to defend one's life when under attack or the claim against being killed by another or the power to sue in the courts for legal protection of one's life or all of these or none of them. His conceptual analysis does not, of course, tell us precisely what the content of this or any other legal right is; only a detailed study of the law of the land can tell us that. What his fundamental legal conceptions do for us is to show us what questions we must ask in order to arrive at a clear understanding of the content of any legal right and to provide us with a terminology in which we can formulate our answers in the most helpful way. There are two very important reasons why it is particularly helpful to define the content of any legal right in Hohfeld's terms. First, such a formulation renders the modality or modalities of any right unambiguous. There is a very real legal difference between a liberty and a claim, or a liberty and a power, or a claim and an immunity. Any vocabulary that does not distinguish between liberty-rights and claim-rights, power-rights and immunity-rights, describes the legal realities inadequately and invites conceptual confusion. Secondly, such a formulation translates the content of any right into practical terms. Each of Hohfeld's fundamental legal conceptions refers to some action. For instance, a

[1] W. N. Hohfeld, *Fundamental Legal Conceptions as Applied in Judicial Reasoning, and other legal essays,* edited by W. W. Cook (New Haven, 1919, reprinted 1923), pp. 35–64.

legal liberty is a liberty to do some action A and a legal power is the power to perform some action with the legal consequence C. Because Hohfeld's conceptions focus upon actions, they are especially appropriate to the law, which regulates and facilitates human actions.

Reflection upon considerations like these has led me to formulate two heuristic principles to guide my investigation of human rights. Since the law has solved the problem of defining the content of its rights better than ethics has, I will take legal rights as my model of human rights. And since Hohfeld provides a terminology for defining legal rights in unambiguous and practical terms, the most theoretically precise and practically fruitful conception of legal rights will be articulated in terms of his fundamental legal conceptions.

Precisely how one can best translate the language of legal rights into Hohfeld's legal advantages is a matter for much debate. Presumably we would like our philosophical analysis of the concept of a legal right to preserve all or most of those features of legal rights we presuppose in our pre-philosophical thinking about them. For one thing, a legal right seems to be permissive for its possessor. In contrast with my legal duty to pay my taxes whether I wish to do so or not, my right to free speech permits, but does not require, me to speak out on controversial political issues. It is this feature that Thomas Hobbes tries to capture by defining a right as a liberty. Again, a legal right of one party imposes one or more duties upon some second party. Thus, the creditor's right to be repaid imposes a duty upon the debtor to repay him. On this model, Wesley Hohfeld identifies a legal right with a legal claim of x against y, the correlative of a corresponding legal duty of y to x. Third, the possessor of any legal right can typically choose to have his right enforced by society. Thomas Holland accordingly defines a legal right as the power of influencing the acts of another by the force of society, specifically through its legal system. The most obvious instance is the legal power of the possessor to sue in the courts for remedy in the event that his right is threatened or violated. Fourth, a legal right is usually secured to its possessor by society. At the very least, the possessor must be legally immune to the annihilation of his right at the mere whim of any second party. Jurists have tended to fasten on one of these features of our thinking about legal rights and build it into their definitions of 'a right', thereby ignoring or rejecting the other aspects of our pre-philosophical thinking. Debate then centres on the issue of which one of these features is most important, even essential, to legal rights. I propose to preserve all four of these features, if I can, because all four are normally taken for granted in our thinking about rights and all four are important in the legal reality to which 'a right' refers. Rather than cut our conception of a legal right down to a single fundamental legal conception, I conceive of a legal right as a cluster of legal liberties, claims, powers, and immunities.

But how can anything as complex as this constitute *a* legal right? What unifies any right is its core. At the centre of any legal right stand one or more legal advantages that define the essential content of the right. Change the core and any remaining right would no longer be this same right. At the core of my right to be repaid is my legal claim to repayment. At the core of my right to free speech is my legal liberty of speaking out on controversial issues. At the core of my right to sell my car is my legal power of transferring ownership in my car to the second party of my choice. When we classify rights as claim-, power- or immunity-rights, it is to their defining cores that we refer. Whatever other legal elements may be contained in any right, they belong to this right because of their relation to its core. Thus, a legal right is not a mere aggregate or collection of disparate legal liberties, claims, powers and immunities; it is a system of legal advantages tied to its defining core.

What are the strings that tie some legal advantage to the core of a right? Upon reflection, it seems to me that every associated liberty, claim, power or immunity contributes some measure of freedom or control over the core to the possessor of the right. Thus, my legal liberty of accepting repayment from the debtor gives me the freedom to cooperate with my debtor should he choose to fulfil my core claim against him. My immunity from having my core claim terminated at the whim of my debtor and my power to sue him should he refuse to repay me both give me control over my legal claim against him, but in different ways. How many such associated elements there are and of what sorts is not a matter to be decided by philosophical analysis; that all depends on the detailed facts of the legal system. Clustered around the core of any legal right, then, are a number of associated legal advantages that give various sorts of freedom and control with respect to that core to the possessor of the right.

Freedom and control are not unrelated; they are two aspects of a single phenomenon. There can be no genuine freedom without control and no real control without freedom. It is not just that I am not free to do or refrain from doing something as long as my action is under the control of others; it is also that my freedom to do or refrain from doing requires that I have some measure of control over their attempts to prevent me from acting or to force me to act against my will. Again, I cannot have control over some part of my life without the freedom to choose and act in this area. Perhaps the most apt label for this totality of freedom and control is 'autonomy' in the sense of self-government. Accordingly, I conceive of a legal right as a system of legal autonomy, a cluster of legal elements that together give its possessor legal freedom with respect to and control over its defining core.

Taking legal rights, thus conceived, as my model, my plan is to develop an analogous conception of human rights. My first step must be to identify and define ethical analogues of Hohfeld's fundamental legal conceptions. Just as he distinguished between legal liberties, claims, powers and immunities, so I hope to define ethical liberties, claims, powers and immunities.

1   *An ethical liberty.* A party has an ethical liberty to perform some action *A* if and only if he does not have any duty not to do *A*. I shall not attempt to define the word 'duty' here, but I do wish to point out that a duty, in the strict sense, must be grounded in specifically moral reasons and that it need not be a duty *to* any assignable second party. I have the ethical liberties of dressing as I please, within the bounds of decency, of spending my spare cash as I wish, and of attending the church of my choice.

2   *An ethical claim.* One party *x* has an ethical claim against some second party *y* that *y* perform some action A if and only if *y* has a duty to *x* to do *A*. Again, I shall leave the word 'duty' undefined, but I must say a word about what makes a duty a duty *to* some second party. A duty is a duty to whoever would be seriously injured by its non-performance. Thus my duty to refrain from striking you is a duty to you because you are the party who would be seriously injured were I to punch you in the nose or kick you in the stomach. Again, my ethical duty to support my child financially is primarily a duty to my child, for it is he who would in the first instance be harmed were I to fail to support him; it may secondarily be a duty to my wife, for she would also suffer seriously were she forced to become both breadwinner and housemother by my failure to perform my duty. Accordingly, you have an ethical claim against me that I not strike you, and my child has an ethical claim against me that I support him.

3   *An ethical power.* A party has the ethical power to bring about some ethical consequence *C* if and only if that party possesses the competence required for performing some act with this ethical consequence. For example, I have the ethical power of making a promise, an act that brings into existence an obligation to do what I have promised, and the promisee has the ethical power to release me from my promise if he so chooses. Notice that not everyone is competent to make promises or release promisees. Children too young to understand what it is to commit themselves to future undertakings cannot promise, even if they have learned to parrot the words 'I promise' in the appropriate linguistic context; similarly, the mentally deranged husband who says to his wife 'I release you from your marriage vows' does not thereby release her from her promise to him. By 'competence' I refer to the qualifications or characteristics one must possess in order that one's action can actually bring about some sort of ethical consequence. What, then, do I mean by 'bringing about an ethical consequence'? To say that some act *A* brings about some ethical consequence *C* is to say that the statement 'act *A* has been done'

implies as a consequence that the ethical statement '*C* is the case' is true. Thus, my act of promising to submit this paper before 1 June brought about my obligation to do so just because 'Carl Wellman promised to submit this paper before 1 June' implies 'Carl Wellman had an obligation to submit this paper before 1 June.' Precisely what kinds of sentences are ethical sentences is a question best left for discussion on another occasion.

4   *An ethical immunity.* A party is immune from some specified ethical consequence *C* if and only if there is no other party who is competent to perform any action with this ethical consequence. For example, I am immune from the loss through any act of another of my ethical claim against second parties that they refrain from striking me and equally immune from being morally bound by promises made by others on my behalf—unless, of course, I have authorized some second party to act for me in such ways.

My next step is to articulate a conception of ethical rights analogous to my conception of legal rights. Just as a legal right is a complex system of legal advantages, so an ethical right is a complex system of ethical advantages, a cluster of ethical liberties, claims, powers and immunities. At the centre of every ethical right stands some unifying core, one or more ethical advantages that define the essential content of the right. Thus, at the centre of my ethical right to dress as I please is my ethical liberty of wearing in public any decent clothing I wish, and the core of my ethical right to equal protection of the laws is my ethical claim against the state that its legal system afford me just as much protection as it affords any other individual subject to it. Around the core of any ethical right cluster an assortment of associated ethical liberties, claims, powers and immunities. What ties these ethical elements together into a single right is the way in which each associated element contributes some sort of freedom or control with respect to the defining core to the possessor of the right. Because freedom and control are two aspects of autonomy, any ethical right can accurately be thought of as a system of ethical autonomy.

My third and last step is to distinguish human rights from other species of ethical rights. It would be at least confusing, and probably an abuse of language, to describe as 'human rights' the ethical rights that any individual human being has by virtue of being a promisee, a wife, or a citizen, for these are not rights one has simply by virtue of being human. Traditionally, human rights have been thought of as those ethical rights that every human being must possess simply because he or she is human. Thus, human rights are the rights any individual possesses *as* a human being. Although this seems to capture current usage pretty well, I propose a more narrow conception of human rights. I define a human right as an ethical right of the individual as human being vis-à-vis the state. Excluded by this definition are the ethical rights one has as a human being that hold against other individuals or against organizations other than the state. I propose this restriction for two reasons. For one thing, all the important human rights documents, and the declarations of natural rights that preceded them, have been essentially political documents; their primary and definitive purpose has traditionally been to proclaim the rights of the individual human being in face of the state. For another thing, the fundamental ethical relations of any individual human being to the state must surely be very different from his or her ethical relations to other individuals just because the state is a special sort of organization with a distinctive role to play in human affairs. Therefore, the ethical rights of an individual against the state will be rather different from his or her rights against other individuals or organizations. To mark this difference I propose to reserve the expression 'a human right' to refer to a right any individual has *as* a human being *in face of* the state.

In three swift steps we have moved from an interpretation of legal rights in terms of Hohfeld's fundamental legal conceptions to a new conception of human rights. A human right is a cluster of ethical liberties, claims, powers and immunities that together constitute a system of ethical autonomy possessed by an individual as a human being vis-à-vis the state. Let me illustrate this new conception by showing how one might use it to interpret the human right to privacy. I shall not pretend to give any complete or precise analysis of this sample right, but my partial description will serve to illustrate a new and helpful way of thinking about human rights.

As the United Nations Declaration of Human Rights recognizes, the core of the human right to privacy is complex. It contains both a claim to freedom from invasions of one's privacy and a claim to legal protection from invasions of one's privacy by the state or other individuals. Both of these are ethical claims of the individual as human being against the state, primarily against his or her own state, but secondarily against other politically organized societies. I would add a third core claim, the ethical claim of the individual against the state that it sustain the conditions necessary for the existence of privacy for the individual.

To define these core claims more fully, it is necessary to say something about the nature of privacy and the areas within which one has justified ethical claims to privacy. Privacy is the state of being unobserved or unknown, confidential, undisturbed or secluded. It is the opposite of being public, and hence the condition of not being open to or shared with the public. One's privacy is invaded when peeping Tom watches one undress, when an entire family must live in a single crowded room, when one's personal letters are published, and when one receives a threatening or obscene telephone call.

Areas within which the claim to privacy are justified include the home, the family, personal correspondence, and certain relationships such as that of husband and wife or doctor and patient. What is it about these areas that singles them out as areas where privacy ought to be respected and protected? In areas such as these, privacy is essential for the preservation of one's sense of security, the development of one's individual personality, and the maintenance of extremely important human relationships. The privacy of the home, for example, is clearly of tremendous value in all three ways: it provides a haven from the dangers, the crowds, and simply the confusions of the public world; it gives one an area where one can be oneself more fully and freely than when subject to alien scrutiny, criticism and even punishment; and it affords an environment in which the intimate relations of husband and wife or parent and child can flourish. The three core claims to privacy are limited to areas where privacy is important in these ways.

Around this complex core cluster a number of associated ethical elements, including at least the following:

1   The ethical liberty of the state to perform its duties corresponding with the three core claims of the individual human being. If the state had any genuine duty not to do these things, then the defining core of the human right to privacy would be vacuous or illusory.

2   The ethical claim of the possessor of the human right to privacy against other individuals that they take political action to ensure that the state perform its duties to meet his core claims. The same considerations that justify the ethical claims of the individual human being concerning privacy against the state justify his claim against other human beings that they intervene on his behalf should the state fail or refuse to perform its core duties to him.

3   The ethical power of the individual to waive his core claims to privacy against the state. For example, it is no longer wrong for a policeman to search a house without a warrant if the owner has freely given his permission to enter and search; and when one marries, one is normally relieving the state of any ethical duty to protect one from invasions of one's privacy by one's spouse.

4   The ethical liberty of the possessor of the right to exercise his ethical power of waiving his core claims to privacy. Although there probably are instances in which one can, but has a duty not to, waive some core claim to privacy, there are many instances in which the exercise of this ethical power is ethically permitted.

5   The ethical immunity of the individual human being against having his core claims to privacy extinguished, suspended or reduced by any action of the state. For example, the state cannot diminish in the least its duty to refrain from invading my privacy by proclaiming a public breakdown of law and order and announcing its intention to search my house or person at any time it sees fit. Each of these

associated ethical elements belong to the human right to privacy because each of them contributes some sort of ethical freedom or control over the core claims to the possessor of that right. Therefore, the core claims together with these, and other, associated elements constitute a system of ethical autonomy with respect to privacy.

I do not insist that my analysis of the human right to privacy is correct in every detail. I do suggest that it illustrates the fruitfulness of a new conception of human rights simply because it is detailed. We tend to speak and think of human rights in terms of mere names or noun phrases that obscure their full and precise content by their very brevity. It is a considerable merit in this conception of a human right that it provides the vocabulary in which one can spell out, explicitly and in detail, the exact content of any right. Another advantage of this conception is that it renders the modality or modalities of any right unambiguous. In this case, it shows us that the core of the human right to privacy is a triple claim and that some associated elements are liberties, others powers and so on. Finally, it translates the content of any human right into practical terms. Since the description of any ethical liberty, claim, power or immunity includes the specification of some sort of action, to think of human rights as clusters of ethical advantages is to think of them in terms of human actions. This is a theoretical virtue for those who believe that the theory of human rights ought to be relevant to moral choice and a practical asset for those who wish to appeal to human rights in taking political action to reform the law to fit a changing society.

5

Human rights—for whom and for what?

Stanley I. Benn

I Human rights—defeasible or absolute?

H. L. A. Hart has distinguished a class of 'general rights' attributable to 'all men capable of choice ... in the absence of those special conditions which give rise to special rights'.[1] 'Special rights' arise from special transactions or relationships. Human rights, if such a class of rights exists, are *general* in Hart's sense. For like the 'natural rights' of an earlier age, human rights are attributable, if at all, to every human being prior to any undertaking into which he may have entered. Though by subsequent deals he may conceivably agree to waive such rights, he enjoys them in the first place independently of his consenting to any contract or covenant, actual or imputed, from which limiting constituent conditions might be inferred. Human rights are enjoyed by all people simply as people, not as participants in agreed practices. Like John Rawls's 'natural duties',[2] they are those that contracting parties in an 'original position' would have reason to acknowledge, but they are not *constituted* by the contract. That is not to say that some social practice may not be a condition for the implementation of such a right. Someone claiming the right to marry as a human right[3] might say that though it has practical application only in a society with marital institutions, it is not membership of such a society that confers the right; no society, once having instituted marital practices, could legitimately confine the right to members of that society, nor could it require that they satisfy any special conditions—say of race, nationality, or religion (and some nowadays

---

[1] 'Are there any Natural Rights?', *Philosophical Review* LXIV (1955), pp. 175–91.
[2] John Rawls, *A Theory of Justice* (Cambridge, Mass., 1971), §19. Rawls says little about natural or human rights.
[3] Universal Declaration of Human Rights (UDHR), 1948, article 16.

would say of sex, too)—not constitutive of the practice as such.[4]

But could any right be so unconditional and universal? All the familiar qualifications—of general welfare, public security, health and so on—suggest that A's human right r is the right of any human being *except under some conditions C*. But in that case, it would evidently not be a sufficient condition for the right that A is human. A familiar response to this objection is the admission that human rights are only *prima facie* rights. A *prima facie* right is not, however, like 'a *prima facie* case'—one that, on further inspection, might be shown not to exist at all, because inadequately grounded. A '*prima facie*' right is perfectly well grounded, but it may be overridden or defeated by some *weightier* consideration.

One of the attractions for liberal individualists of the consensual theory of political authority is that it offers a legitimation of those restrictions of general rights that seem practically unavoidable. If A's natural right r is overridden by public safety condition C, one can comfort oneself that anyone consenting to government waives r in any C; and on the assumption that the power of waiver is in any case a constituent of r, C is not really a defeating or an overriding condition, but one that actually implements that very power. When A says to B, 'Don't bother to pay me the \$100 you owe me', his right to \$100 is indeed extinguished, but by the exercise of a power that is a constituent (and, some would say, a *necessary* constituent) of the right-relationship. For if A were obliged to accept B's \$100, it might seem more appropriate to say he had a power and a duty to exact it (like a tax collector), rather than a right to it.

Such arguments, however, are generally unsatisfactory. If they are intended to legitimize actual political and legal restrictions on natural or human rights, they have to show that the individuals concerned really have agreed to such restrictions. If they maintain, more radically, that individuals have not agreed, the consequences are not likely to be acceptable, except perhaps to an anarchist. If, however, the consensual theory is offered only as a model of what it would be rational for individuals to agree to, under some specified conditions presenting them with a coordination problem,[5] it cannot be assumed that actual individuals, who may never have been in that condition, or who may be less than rational, have indeed waived the rights in question. A model is an 'as-if' device: it may be heuristically apt, but unless its postulates can be shown to be satisfied in the essential respects, it can neither

---

[4] Note, however, that article 12 of the European Convention for the Protection of Human Rights and Fundamental Freedoms (ECPHR), 1950 qualifies the right of 'men and women of marriageable age' to marry 'according to the national laws governing the exercise of this right'. This right would be consistent with apartheid marriage laws.

[5] Cf. Robert Goodin, *The Politics of Rational Man* (London and New York, 1976), p. 198.

explain nor justify. It is not enough that the model generates results corresponding closely to the *explananda* or *justificanda*.

In any case, the point of human rights doctrine has generally been to provide a legitimation not of political authority but of claims against tyrannical or exploiting regimes. If the doctrine is to keep any cutting edge, therefore, it must permit us to say that human rights *survive* political association, rather than that political association extinguishes such of them as are necessary for its purposes.

A partial solution is that a right defeated or overridden is not necessarily a right lost. The practice of compensation when private property is compulsorily purchased by public authorities is a recognition that, though considerations of public interest may override a person's right to decide how to dispose of his own property, they do not thereby extinguish his rights in the matter. The right of which he is deprived must be made up to him in some other way, or he suffers injustice. But of course the imprisonment, or the killing, of criminals is not like that. The right to life or liberty is held forfeit, not just overridden by a stronger consideration.

The classic declarations of human rights, issuing generally from compromise between a vision of a free and just future and a sharp awareness of the political hazards of an unstable present, have hedged their bold affirmations of right with cautious escape clauses. Consider article 8 of the European Convention for the Protection of Human Rights and Fundamental Freedoms:

1   Everyone has the right to respect for his private and family life, his home and his correspondence.

2   There shall be no interference by a public authority with the exercise of this right except such as is in accordance with the law and is necessary in a democratic society in the interests of national security, public safety or the economic well-being of the country, for the prevention of disorder or crime, for the protection of health or morals, or for the protection of the rights and freedoms of others.

The qualifying form of words in the second paragraph suggests that while the right is not extinguished, it may properly be overridden by certain weightier and very broadly specified considerations. Similar phrases occur in articles 9, 10, and 11, qualifying the rights of freedom of thought, conscience and religion, freedom of expression, of peaceful assembly and association, including the right to join trade unions. Even so fundamental a right as the right to life (article 2) is qualified to permit capital punishment imposed lawfully by a court as a penalty for a crime. Yet why, if such rights are *human* rights, should someone's being guilty of a crime deny him the enjoyment of them? Do people enjoy such rights as men and women, or only as well behaved men and women—*quamdiu se bene gesserint*? If criminal behaviour can extinguish any human right, does it extinguish all? And how much criminality is required for this to happen? And if not all are extinguished, how to decide which? This is not a purely theoretical question: it is forcefully posed by proposals for compulsory psycho-surgery and conditioning therapy for criminals, including sterilization for sexual offenders. Many people who object to such treatment as an invasion of the criminal's human rights would not object on the same grounds to imprisoning him.

II The telé of human rights

A possible way to maintain the universality of human rights is to try to specify with some precision what conditions would defeat a claim to a human right; or to put it more accurately, so to define the right that what belongs absolutely to any human being is the right only to have or do what is not excluded by such conditions. The right to whatever is excluded would not then be overridden; rather, it would never have existed. Article 5 of the European Convention, dealing with the right to liberty and security of persons, proceeds rather in this way: having stated the general principle, it enumerates six fairly precise conditions, (the lawful detention of a person to prevent the spread of infectious disease is one instance) which nullify the right. The framers of declarations of rights could never be happy, however, that all excluding conditions had been specified. Defeasibility is open ended.[6] So they fall back on generalities and catch-all phrases that blunt the cutting edge of a declaration. For unless some systematic and intelligible principle can be elicited from the exclusions already accepted, what is to count as a reason for admitting further excluding conditions? And to say of such a principle that it is 'intelligible' would be to say that there is a reason why a right under the excluded condition could not belong to anyone simply *qua* human being.

Instead of assuming that human beings have a given right, and then trying to draw up lists of *ad hoc* excluding conditions, it may be more promising to ask why a given right is to be attributed to them at all. For then we may be able to reconcile the right with some at least of the excluding conditions, on the grounds that these limitations do not interfere with the *telos* of the right. I mean by the *telos* of a right whatever it is for the sake of which the right exists, that gives point to ascribing it. I prefer not to speak of the *purpose* or *end* for which it exists, for that smacks too exclusively of consequentialism. Some rights may be ascribed because the consequences are generally good; but some may have a different kind of point, having to do, for instance, with respect owed to persons.

[6] See Hart, *op. cit.*

Professor Carl Wellman, earlier in this volume, has drawn our attention to the structural complexity of human rights: each complex right, he asserts, clusters around a core right which identifies the nature and contents of the set; this one is what all the other powers, claims, privileges, and immunities are all about. I doubt, however, whether selecting one from the complex set of rights is the best way of comprehending their structural unity. Rather, we can talk of a particular complex as, for instance, *the* right to privacy, because there is a common *telos*, or a group of related *telé*, that explain why this power and that liberty must be included in the right, while some other one can be left out.

The right to privacy is a particularly good example to work with, because, as a relative newcomer, it is still not very well defined, and in order to make its way it has to thrust aside other well established rights, such as the rights of free enquiry and free reporting. In doing so, it compels us to examine not only the importance of privacy itself, but also the point of the rights it challenges. Moreover, in the case of privacy, three distinct kinds of *telé* are distinguishable in the literature and case law, and it is questionable whether the same complex is required by each one. The first is related to the conception of moral personality and individuality, to a person's need for freedom from intrusion in order to manage his own internal psychic economy and to manage and cultivate his relations with other persons. The second relates to freedom, to the fact that someone able to assemble a great deal of information about another person almost certainly acquires a measure of power over him. The third relates to commercial or proprietorial interests, such as the interest a professional sportsman or film actor may have in controlling advertisers' use of his likeness or reputation. If we were to explore these notions in depth, we should get a better grasp of what interests a human right of privacy would protect, and what claims to privacy can be set aside without prejudicing the idea of human personality to which, I believe, the notion primarily relates. Conversely, in assessing the claims of press reporters to inquire and report freely, it makes good sense to ask what the *telos* of this right may be; to what extent would it be impaired, for instance, were the right to publish details of someone's illness so restricted that the patient could not easily be identified? And if exceptions to the restriction were allowed in respect, say, of occupiers of, or candidates for, high public offices, would the right to privacy be lost so long as the subject could continue to enjoy it by resigning or withdrawing his candidature? And just as slander is an abuse of the right of free speech, because that isn't what the right is all about, so privacy to batter one's wife or child is not what the privacy of the home is all about. It is not so much that the rights of the victim override the right to privacy of the batterer; it is rather that the batterer's invalid claim to privacy is parasitic on a valid claim based on a human interest in cultivating personal family relations. Bashing children is not a way to do that. So it is undermined by a fuller account of the interests claiming protection.

I do not propose, however, to explore in detail the *telé* of any human right in particular, though it is to that kind of study that I want to point the way. I shall suggest instead that there are three fundamental moral propositions on which a schema for rationalizing human rights can be erected, which would show us where to look for their *telé*, and suggest a way of testing whether a given claim that such a right existed could be justified. The three propositions are:

1 that natural persons ought to be respected, as moral persons;

2 that human beings are objects of value;

3 that certain directions of human development are desirable, and that certain qualities are human excellences.

These propositions are not all of the same type. The first is deontological, the second two are axiological. Since the notion of a right belongs, in my view, to deontological rather than to axiological ethics, it will be necessary to show how the latter can generate rights at all. Because Dr Kleinig anchors his account of human rights only in the axiological notion of welfare, he fails, in my view, to give an adequate account of the moral difference between harming things of value in general and *wronging* human persons in particular by denying them their rights.

III Rights as reasons for action or forbearance

A person's duties are reasons for him to act or to forbear, whether he wants to or not. A person's rights are reasons for someone else to act or forbear; so too, however, are someone's needs, his pain, his deserts, and possibly his merits. How then are rights distinct from other reasons for action, and in particular, reasons constituted by the welfare needs of valuable objects like human beings, hens, works of art, or forests?

1 Wellman, following Hart, points to the power of waiver as a distinguishing characteristic of a right. If *A* has a right to be paid $100 by *B*, *B* has a (legal or moral) reason to pay *A* $100, unless *A* extinguishes that reason by waiver. A right is thus a normative resource,[7] a capacity to constitute a reason for action for other persons, as it suits one's own interests and projects. In the case of a liberty, it

[7] Richard Wasserstrom calls human rights 'moral commodities'. See his 'Rights, Human Rights, and Racial Discrimination', *Journal of Philosophy* LXI (1964), pp. 628–41.

amounts to a ground for rejecting considerations advanced by someone else as reasons for desisting from such projects. Rights are therefore at least freedom-constituting, at most opportunity-creating. In this respect they differ from reasons of need, which are simply welfare-promoting.

2   To fail in one's duty *in respect of* someone is to be morally or legally delinquent, but it is not always to do an injury *stricto sensu* (*injuria*). The man who fell among thieves was worse off than he would have been had either the priest or the Levite done his duty, but though they failed in their Good Samaritan duties they did not do him a *wrong*; he had no right (*jus*) to their good works. One may have a duty to act generously towards one's business competitors, but the duty is not a duty *to* them, and they have no ground for grievance if, using only fair business practices, one drives them into bankruptcy. The duty is a reason for action (or forbearance), but not one that the bankrupt could manipulate as a normative resource, like a contractual right. Of course, the man who fell among thieves would have had no less justification than generations of Christians since in condemning the priest and the Levite for their failure in charity; but though he felt it most directly and acutely, he had no special kind of reproach, no standing in the matter different from that of anyone else. By contrast, someone whose *rights* are withheld would have in addition a justifiable grievance and grounds for resentment. For injury constitutes a failure in justice, not in mercy or in benevolence, a failure to render what is due, not merely a failure to do what it would be good or best to do because the consequences would be the best. Injury, in this strict sense, has to do with fairness. One need not consider the question of fairness in giving presents to one's friends. But if present-giving is required by a role, as when we give Christmas presents to our children or our office staff, *A* suffers an injury if his present is not as good as *B*'s, there being no relevant difference between them.

This isn't merely a question of formal rationality. It is irrational, or at best non-rational, to treat any like objects differently. For instance, because there are the same good reasons for keeping two equally fine and precious paintings in an air-conditioned room, or for feeding all one's battery hens the same laying pellets, it would be irrational, other things being equal, to favour this and neglect that. If, besides, one gave some of the hens no food at all, one would then be not only irrational but morally delinquent too, because cruel—but still not guilty of injustice. Suppose, however, that *A* is not a hen but a human person. If he differs from *B* in no relevant respect, he may have a *right* to be treated as favourably, and if he is not, he may have grounds not merely for chagrin, disappointment, annoyance, and condemnation, but also for resentment. So if the social decision processes work so that *A* gets too little food and *B* too much, we may be inclined to say not merely that the system is irrational or bad, like a picture gallery whose administration neglects its pictures, or cruel, like a careless poultry farmer, but unjust—that *A* is not merely harmed, but wronged or injured by it. And that is not because human beings are to be valued more highly than hens or pictures, so that the consequences are more deplorable if they get less than they need to keep them in good condition. There is an additional delinquency of a totally different kind.

The distinction to which I am directing attention is that between deontological and axiological grounds for actions and for appraisals of actions and institutions. What is it, then, about human beings such that neglecting their well-being can raise questions of justice and right, and not merely of moral goodness?

IV Human rights as the rights of natural persons

It is a mistake, in my view, to make the distinction hinge on the difference between *human* beings and others: it is not their humanity, a simple biological characteristic having no necessary moral implications, but their personality that makes the crucial difference between right-bearers and other objects. The *natural personality* of nearly all human beings consists in their having a certain kind of self-awareness, a conception of themselves as initiators of actions that make a difference to the course of events. They are conceptually equipped to envisage alternative possibilities, to prefer one state to another, and to decide on a course of action intended to bring about one in preference to another. Moreover, each not only knows himself as such a person, but also distinguishes himself and his initiatives from other similar persons and theirs. This characteristic may not be confined to human beings: some chimpanzees educated by human teachers have shown a conceptualizing capacity that may extend to this kind of self-conceptualization; it is possible that intelligent dogs or dolphins may have it, or be capable of learning it from human beings. On the other hand, there are some human beings who do not have it; congenital idiocy or brain damage could deprive one of it. Yet it is so nearly universal a feature of human beings that the generalization that human beings are natural persons is pragmatically reasonable, at least as a rule of thumb.

A person knowing himself to be a person in a world of persons is aware that they, like him, have projects important to them, and that his actions may impair theirs as theirs often impair his. This may be no more than a grim fact of life; he may take what evasive action he can, and regret the mess when it fails. On the other hand, he may come to feel that people who understand very well what it is to have their own projects spoiled by the carelessness and unconcern of others ought to have some respect for his—and for him as their author. And he may resent their trampling on these projects without a thought, and, even more, their treating him as a mere impediment or as an instrument for their own projects, as though he had none of his own that mattered. And if his resentment were grounded in their failure to appreciate what in his view any person ought to be able to grasp in his dealings with another person, he would be supposing a general moral principle—that of respect for natural persons. This amounts to saying that any natural person is also a moral person, a bearer of rights, which constitute for any other person reasons (though not necessarily conclusive reasons) for forbearance in respect of his projects.

From this basic deontological notion of respect for persons, which has nothing whatsoever to do with valuing them, derives a set of very general principles that include, for example:

1 The principle of non-interference—that there is an onus of justification resting on any person who proposes to act in a way that will frustrate or constrain the projects of another person.[8]

2 The principle of equal consideration—that discrimination in treatment between persons requires *moral* justification: it is not enough simply to *prefer* one to another, since that involves regarding another person solely from the point of view of one's own satisfactions; respect for a person involves recognizing his right to be considered from his *own* standpoint.

3 At a slightly less abstract level, it follows that if a legal order is to exist to regulate relations between natural persons, no natural person can be denied a capacity for legal rights, since their *telos* is to provide natural persons with institutional normative resources to safeguard their capacities for selecting and pursuing their own projects.

To these three classical Kantian principles I would add:

4 That because *A* as a person has a conception of himself, and is not *only* an object of perceptions, to observe him, report on him, participate in his activieties for one's own purposes, without considering what significance such observation and so on would have for him as a subject, is to treat him without the respect due to a person. This principle shifts from *A* to *B* the onus of justification implied in the principle of non-interference that would otherwise leave *B* free to observe, report and so on on anything whatsoever, unless *A* could provide reason to the contrary. Were this shift not to take place, there

---

[8] For a fuller argument on the connection between natural personality, moral personality, respect for persons and the principle of non-interference, see my 'Freedom, Autonomy and the Concept of a Person', *Proceedings of the Aristotelian Society* LXXVI (1976), pp. 109–30. See also my paper 'Personal Freedom and Environmental Ethics: the Moral Inequality of Species' in *Equality and Freedom: International and Comparative Jurisprudence*, edited by G. Dorsey (3 vols, New York and Leiden, 1977) II, pp. 401–24, for a fuller account of my reasons for confining rights to natural persons, and for the distinction between deontological and axiological reasons for action.

would be nothing objectionable in *B*'s using *A*, whether *A* agreed to it or not, as an object of amusement, like a performing flea, as an object of curiosity, like a geophysicist's bit of moon rock, or as an object of appreciation, perhaps for admiration, as a connoisseur might regard a picture. None of these attitudes would be consistent with the respect due from one person to another.

These principles are so broad that they hardly qualify as rights; they are rather rules of procedure in justificatory discourse. For that very reason one can say with confidence that they apply universally and without qualification to all persons. Nevertheless, they do yield some principles that can properly be expressed as human rights. For instance, though there is nothing in these principles to prohibit punishment for crimes, the principle of respect for persons provides grounds for a right not to be punished under retroactive laws, nor to be the victim of unexpectedly severe 'exemplary' penalties for the sake of deterring others. It seems reasonable to regard both practices as unfair, and as failing in respect, since the victim is singled out as a lever for manipulating the behaviour of others, regardless of his standing as a natural person with a point of view deserving of consideration, and with projects claiming the forbearance of other persons. In the standard instance of criminal penalties, by contrast, the offender is punished for what he has knowingly chosen, from among options which are admittedly weighted to make some less attractive than others. Such weighting is, of course, a constraint upon freedom of action;[9] whether we see it as infringing a human right would depend on the action, for the principle of non-interference is not an absolute licence to do whatever you like, but a liberty to do what there is not a good reason for your being prevented from doing.

But though these broad principles yield only very general procedural rights, they provide forms too which, when supplemented with judgements of value, can yield very much more substantial rights. Indeed, principles like these can account for the difference between a duty not to be cruel to hens, or not to vandalize works of art, and duties not merely to respect persons, but to deal fairly and justly with them in matters concerning their well-being—to acknowledge not only their human needs but their human rights.

V Human beings as valuable objects

I have coined the term *axiotimon* to refer to 'something it is appropriate to value or esteem', distinguishing the concept *axiotimon* from that of a person, properly an object of respect and forbearance.[10] It would be

---

[9] See S. I. Benn and W. L. Weinstein, 'Being Free to Act and Being a Free Man', *Mind* LXXX (1971), pp. 194–211.

[10] 'Personal Freedom and Environmental Ethics', *op. cit.*

irrational, other things being equal, to regard something as an *axiotimon*, but not to care whether it exists or not, flourishes or decays. To all *axiotima*, therefore, can be ascribed needs—conditions necessary if the object is to remain that by virtue of which it is valued; for something valued as a racehorse would no longer be valued as a corpse. The word 'welfare' is usually used only of human beings, or, at the broadest, of the higher mammals, but the concept of welfare seems to me just as applicable to inanimate objects like pictures which need to be cared for, for which concern can be properly felt and displayed, as to animals. And it is evident that in so far as any object is an *axiotimon*, its welfare needs constitute moral reasons for action, or at least for forbearance, for people in a position to do something about them.

Human beings, no less than pictures, racehorses, or trees, are *axiotima*. This is the second of the moral propositions suggested in section III, above. For the purpose of this chapter, I take it as a moral datum. Elsewhere, I have offered reasons that seem to me persuasive, though not rationally compelling, for accepting this datum.[11] The conditions without which they could not live, or retain the features by virtue of which we perceive them as *axiotima*, I shall call their 'basic needs'. Where these are not otherwise being supplied, they constitute for any moral person reasons for action. Failing to act on such reasons may be a failure of charity or benevolence; but should it also be seen as a denial of right, and if so, why?

There is no doubt, that—as Kleinig points out—recent declarations include social and economic rights, such as 'the right to a standard of living adequate for the health and well-being' of a person and his family, 'including food, clothing, housing and medical care'. The change that has occurred since the earliest declarations of the rights of man is that what was then seen only as the material of duties of benevolence—to care for the poor and the unfortunate, according to what one could reasonably spare from one's own more extensive need, for instance—is now the material content of the rights of the poor. It is not completely clear where the correlative duty lies; some people would say that we all have a duty to one another; others would say that it rests upon the state. I doubt, however, whether that would be, without qualification, a satisfactory account. On the one hand, if, for instance, everyone were getting a perfectly satisfactory education from religious bodies and voluntary agencies, would the state be failing in a duty to meet the human right to education? On the other hand, if despite the efforts of a given state to meet the basic needs of its people, they still starved, while other people elsewhere ate to excess, would it be altogether absurd to say that this was unjust, and that the human rights of the needy were being denied them?

[11] *ibid.*

The change in outlook is to be accounted for, I think, by seeing it as a convergence of axiological and deontological considerations. If human beings were *only* objects of value, then the moral language of benevolence would be adequate to account for our duties; and this was sufficient for medieval Christian theology. The new development was the individualism of seventeenth-century England and its American colonies—epitomized in Colonel Rainborough's 'the poorest he that is in England hath a life to live as the greatest he', amounting to an assertion of the moral personality of every English natural person. The personal rights of, for instance, the Declaration of the Rights of Man, are a political version of the rights to equal consideration and non-interference.

The second stage was the growth of public responsibility for welfare services in the economically developed nations of the West. Public assistance in earlier centuries, whether administered by monasteries or by the parish vestry, could still be seen as a way in which the private duty of benevolence of the wealthier classes was conveniently institutionalized. But once everyone, as a moral person, had a right to vote, and economic management and income redistribution became a regular and recognized feature of state policy, everyone's need became a subject of claims on state consideration, a matter for just distribution, not simply a natural consequence of social laws, like the laws of supply and demand, the rigours of which were to be mitigated by charitable giving. If it was within the power of a government to treat its GNP as a pool, from which resources could be allocated to meet social needs, the poor were getting less than their due if, at the very least, their basic needs were not being met. For, to echo Colonel Rainborough, they were as much persons as the rich, and therefore entitled to equal consideration. It might be shown, perhaps, that equal distribution of the whole pool would have disincentive effects and so reduce the net amount available for distribution, but unless there was at least equality in distribution to meet basic needs before anything was made available for luxuries, the poor, as *axiotima*, could legitimately complain that they were receiving less consideration than others—that their existence was being less highly prized than that of other similar *axiotima*—and that this amounted to a denial of their moral right as persons to be considered equally with all other persons.

Human welfare rights arise, then, not directly from a right that needs—even basic needs—should be satisfied, but rather from a right to equal consideration and fair treatment. If anyone's needs are to be satisfied, then no one's need for the less basic goods should be satisfied before everyone's need for the most basic, since we are all alike *axiotima*. We have grounds for resentment at being deprived when others do well—not at having too little *tout court*.

From a doctrine imposing the duty to satisfy the human rights of its citizens upon each state, it is a short step to holding mankind corporately responsible for human rights everywhere, and to asserting the rights of poorer states to the help of the wealthier so that the needs of their poorer citizens can be met. While international aid began as benevolence, it is increasingly claimed as of right.

VI Rights to conditions of excellence

So far I have confined the notion of need to the conditions necessary to preserve *axiotima*—and particularly human beings. Unlike pictures, however, human beings have a capacity for development. It is possible, therefore, to assign value to them not only as biological objects, but as beings achieving varying degrees of excellence, and admirable in proportion to their achievement. If we focus on that variation in achievement, we shall be led away from human rights, as was Nietzsche, to the rights of superman. But if we focus instead on the many and varied forms of excellence towards which human beings can aspire and, in particular, on the excellence peculiar to a moral person—autonomy—the argument for a human right to basic needs can develop into a right to the conditions for the attaining of whatever excellence a person is capable of. These would presumably include the UDHR rights to education, to leisure, and to participate in the cultural life of the community.[12]

I have argued elsewhere[13] that someone who attached importance to his ontological status as a natural person would have a reason for valuing autonomy—the condition of being one's own man, of having a disposition to act on a set of principles, standards, and values that one has made one's own, by a process of critical exploration and resolution of the incoherences of the plural tradition into which one has been socialized. I believe, with Kleinig (if I interpret him correctly), that the ideal of autonomy, of responsibility for oneself, is the *telos* of that set of human rights that have to do with freedom, especially freedom of thought and expression, and of that nexus of rights that are aimed against unreasonable detention, interference with free movement and forms of political oppression generally. Autonomy requires conditions in which criticism can flourish, in which a person can discover, from the open confrontation of ideals within his society—of Christian brotherhood, say, and racial supremacy—where he stands and what he is. From a deeper exploration of the concept of autonomy we can derive, perhaps, a more coherent understanding of such rights, of their extent and of any limiting conditions set by their *telos*. For instance, since autonomy, so far from being lawlessness, consists in being the author of one's own *nomos*, it is important to know whether there are

[12] UDHR, articles 26, 24 and 27.
[13] See my 'Freedom, Autonomy, and the Concept of a Person', *op. cit.*

(as Kant believed) limiting conditions that a *nomos* will need to satisfy to be one that a person can rationally acknowledge as his own. For those conditions might then constrain the freedoms that constitute human rights, without the sacrifice of universality, thereby helping to solve the problem that generated the present inquiry.

VII Human rights and community virtues

The extension of the notion of human rights from basic needs to rights to the opportunities for achieving human excellences opens up an enormous range of problems into which I cannot venture. It is not, however, that there are diverse human ideals, each with its own excellences. That objection could be accommodated by a pluralist conception of excellence—there are many roads, and everyone must find his own. The problems arise when one person's excellence is another person's shortcoming.

Kleinig has pointed to such a problem in querying whether 'rights-talk' would be apposite in a community which exhibited love and concern for one another. A capacity for such relations clearly ranks high in Kleinig's canon of excellences, and though he smiles benignly on autonomy, he does not relate it to these *Gemeinschaft* ideals. I believe, however, that Kleinig is mistaken, or at any rate his form of words is misleading, when he asserts: 'Where people do love and care for each other, there is no need for recourse to rights-talk, since what is due to the other will be encompassed within the loving or caring relationship.'[14] Love and care can be stifling and crippling, unless they are associated with respect, and with the recognition that the loved object is also a person, with projects of his own which deserve forbearance. The most benevolent paternalism puts the 'father's' purpose for the 'child' above that of the child for himself, no matter how loving the father's purpose may be. If there is no need for rights-*talk* where love and respect are conjoined, it is because respectful love acknowledges the loved one's rights, forbearing as well as cherishing. There is no need for expressions of claims, grievances, and resentment, the characteristic contexts of 'rights-talk', because no rights are then denied. But the absence of talk, even of consciousness of rights, should not be taken to show that rights are irrelevant or unimportant to such relations, or that they are not acknowledged and respected. On the contrary, the reflective beloved may well perceive with gratitude that his lover is sensitively alert to make such protests unnecessary. *Gemeinschaft* is not a single species: it is a spectrum, ranging from a totalitarian group concern that makes total submission to the prevailing group ideal the price of its love, to a caring association

---

[14] Above, p. 46.

of autonomous persons engaged in the creation and development of a mutuality, in which each remains secure in his own freedom, freely conceding to the others what is due to them as persons, confident that they will take pride and joy in doing the same for him, as an expression not merely of love but of respect too.

6

Analyses of right

Christopher Arnold

I

We construct a theory in the face of a problem or a set of problems. The direction of theory to problems is true in all cases, but is most often seen in the case of logical theory. In logic, we offer canonical translations of a language to reveal just enough of the structure of its sentences to cope with the problems in hand—to block any paradox or to explain certain inferences—and no more. We do not, for instance, raise the doubt whether we really can know anything in constructing a modal logic of knowledge.

Analysis at this level simply involves logical progress and not necessarily any other kind of progress. It is not to trivialize logic to say that the maxim of limited analysis applies; it is just to recognize that a theory—any theory—is a function of a certain problem or set of problems.

II Rights as primitives

In legal theory the maxim of limited analysis also applies when we exhibit the logical scaffolding supporting a legal system. Our theoretical concerns here are to organize familiar features of law into a simple and logical model, and to elucidate basic concepts, like property or right, in the light of that model. What is puzzling is to grasp the necessary features of law to portray a minimum structure. We feel that there are differences between legal systems and other systems of regulation but it is notoriously difficult to assemble the basic items perspicuously and logically. In exposing the scaffolding of law and legal concepts, however, we do not need to be concerned with the nature and point of our concepts; it is enough at this level to record those elements in a rigorous model.

One of the neatest ways with the perplexities of general structure is to begin with legal processes and with the specialities of legal arguments.[1] It is typical of law that there is the possibility, at some stage, of taking legal action to settle a matter. Legal action, if pursued far enough, will involve adjudication by a judge. Judicial adjudication is the characteristically legal method of settling matters; it allows officials to fix, once and for all, the entitlements and liabilities of those in dispute. Any settlement of issues in law involves a public declaration of those entitlements and liabilities upon facts which have been proved. But the judicial process of adjudication is not random; we need to refer, at some stage, to acceptable public standards—acceptable in terms of their formal ancestry—as crucial steps in the arguments by which liabilities are eventually fixed by officials. Argument from authority in this formal sense is also typical of a legal process; it distinguishes law from a wholly discretionary system and from a system in which the only rule is that might is always right. In addition we expect official machinery in support of any public declaration. If at the end of the day it were left to litigants to settle the executions of judgements, then the appeal to formal authorities as part of the process may well have been pointless. Only by the presence of official machinery in support do we guarantee that appeal to formal authorities will not be overcome later, by discretion or by might.

In this neat picture the familiar elements of law are related around a central idea that law may be equated with good reasons for a judicial decision upon entitlements and liabilities. Those other features—the presence of authoritative criteria and the institutional paraphernalia in support—supplement that central idea. Individual legal concepts such as property and personality can now be defined within that model, by reference to the reasoning processes of the system. The swiftness with which I have portrayed that logical model should not mask my admiration for it. Everything familiar to us is caught through the particular aspect of legal reasoning; analysis at this level then becomes a function of the relations each element has with every other element in the process of reasoning.

Within such a scheme the greatest weight is borne by the concepts of right and duty. They have something like the role of undefined primitives for the system, serving as foundation for all the rest. The analogy is again with logical theory. We can accept there a number of undefined primitives; the remaining apparatus is then explained in terms of the primitives to complete the logic. When, in law, we ask for an analysis of the notions of right and duty themselves, however, we receive a limited reply. They can be elucidated only by reference to each other and to the rest of the scaffolding they support. On those

[1] For an introduction to this way of thinking about law, see G. Calabresi and A. D. Melamed, 'Property Rules, Liability Rules, and Inalienability: One View of the Cathedral', *Harvard Law Review* LXXXV (1971–2), pp. 1089–128 at pp. 1089–92.

terms a logic of relations, of right and duty, is a possible enterprise.

It is quite revealing to understand the role of rights and duties as primitives and to see how they enter logically into every other relation from the bottom to the top. The elucidation of rights and duties themselves rests upon two features. First, since the formal standards of any system of law tend to operate generally, individual statement of right and duty appear as consequences following from the application of general standards to facts. In their case there is an argument process with individual right as a conclusion.[2] Secondly, right and duty are connected to each other as correlatives. The concept of a right is fully unravelled in the idea of 'a right against another', that is to say as a right to some service from another person or group of persons. Duty in turn is fully unravelled in the idea of 'a duty towards another', that is to say as a duty to act for the benefit of another person or group of persons. So duty looks to advantages and right looks to disadvantages. Right and duty are thus two different ways of describing some single three-termed relation between different people,[3] seen now as one man's burden, seen now as another man's benefit. It is a single relation since there is just one relation tying individuals and services together in each case.

This is as much as can be achieved by way of logical analysis within the confines of the model. It counts as analysis and theory in this sense. A general problem of portraying a model has been set. The neat way of tackling this problem was to set up two ideas as primitives and to simplify the rest of the system with their help. And it is quite revealing, as I said earlier, to have pointed out the special logical connection that legal rights and duties have with standards of a public kind and with each other.

To those general features may be added in the case of legal rights familiar details of judical doctrine which tend to separate legal rights from the other rights. Recourse to judicial doctrine is a legitimate additional strategy in analysis. If rights are elucidated against a background of legal standards, then judicial doctrine about rights, within those standards, will supply important additional structure. Judicial doctrine supplies two ideas. In the first place there is acceptance of the idea that rights and duties are significant only in terms of the addition of a remedy or sanction. Thus, as one judge has put it:[4]

> If a duty is prescribed but no remedy for its breach is imposed, it can be assumed that a right of civil action accrues . . . for, if it were not so, the statute would be but a pious aspiration.

[2] H. L. A. Hart, 'Definition and Theory in Jurisprudence', *Law Quarterly Review* LXX (1954), pp. 37–60.

[3] See A. R. Anderson, 'Logic, Norms, and Roles', *Ratio* IV (1962), pp. 36–49.

[4] *Cutler* v. *Wandsworth Stadium* [1949] A.C.398 at 407. See also *Attorney-General* v. *St Ives Rural District Council* [1960] 1 Q.B.312.

With us legal rights become rights of action and the aspect of redress supports the formal idea that the legal process is not merely a declaratory process. Of course, there are borderline cases of legal rights without remedies; there are so-called unenforceable rights and declarations are sometimes given without supporting relief. But we can tolerate these at the periphery without assault on general judicial doctrine. There could not be a legal system in which all rights were unenforceable or in which the judicial process always halted at a declaration. Then it would be difficult to see anything remaining in the idea of legal right as opposed to moral right.

In the second place, judicial doctrine reveals an ambiguity in the term 'rights'. It is clear that the notion of a legal right covers, in addition to the case of rights against another, the case of a right or a liberty to perform an action. Lawyers have been well served by theorists,[5] who have pointed out that in the cases judges recognize (though not always without confusion) legal rights which are liberties protected by general duties against interference. There is, then, a difference between 'someone's having a right to do something', and 'someone's having a right against someone else'. And this is masked by the ambiguous phrase, 'having a right'. The ambiguity is dissolved by the corresponding correlatives—in the distinction between 'a duty to perform some service for another's benefit', and 'a duty not to interfere with another's activity'.

Thus judicial doctrine supplements the logic of right in these ways. In the logical analysis of concepts the prevailing feature of a legal right is that the concept of a legal right is a precise one. We might say then that in its logic, in its role as a primitive for the rest of the scaffolding, the concept of legal right is finely drawn.

III Redundancy of rights

There are good reasons to feel that analysis of the kind exemplified above does not exhaust theoretical inquiries. It is after all a limited enterprise in the face of perplexities of a logical kind. In the case of right, problems of another kind exist. For instance, we may be concerned to ask what sort of thing a right is, and what its general point and role is. We need not go into this concern in constructing a logic of relations but we do need to ask this question if we are interested in fundamental matters.[6]

---

[5] On liberties, see the useful account of Hohfeld by T. D. Perry, 'A Paradigm of Philosophy: Hohfeld on Legal Rights', *American Philosophical Quarterly* XIV (1977), pp. 41–50.

[6] On the different levels of analysis, see J. O. Urmson, *Philosophical Analysis* (Oxford, 1956), chapter 4, pp. 45–53 and W. Quine, *Word and Object* (New York and London, 1960), chapter 6, §45.

Suppose, to start, we were engaged in giving a general description of the kinds of items that exist in the world, making a general inventory of the world's furniture. We might accept the presence of spatio-temporal objects, and of events, and perhaps of classes. Within that general scheme we might raise the question, where rights and duties fit in. They do not obviously belong to any such general categories. We might therefore introduce relations and try to reduce rights to kinds of behaviour as relations. If we are puzzled about what relations are, we might try to throw light on this general category by giving other examples of relations. Now among relations, consider various non-symmetric and non-reflexive relations like 'being the parent of' or 'being to the left of' and of course 'having a right against'. All those relations have corresponding relations such as 'being the child of' and 'being to the right of' and of course 'having a duty towards'. What is puzzling about these relations is why we need in each case the double description of a single relation. Descriptions of the world could be satisfactorily made with one half only of the correlated pair. No relation for instance of 'being the child of' or of 'being to the right of' could possibly exist which could not be adequately accounted for by the alternative language of 'being a parent of' and 'being to the left of'. We could raise the question therefore, if we were concerned to give a general description of the world including relations, why for various relations we tolerate correlatives or double descriptions. If the pairs genuinely correlate then one description would seem to be eliminable without loss. Of course the paired relations do not mean the same. Each relation in the formula aRb is looked at first from the point of view of a and then of b. But they are correlatives; no more information is conveyed by the expression 'X is the parent of Y' than is conveyed by the corresponding expression 'Y is the child of X.'

If we turn our attention to legal relations, could it not be argued that, notwithstanding its place in any logic, in fact, the notion of a right is not necessary? It is correlated to the notion of a duty which adequately describes the three-termed relation in law. It is worth putting the thesis about elimination this way round, in terms of the redundancy of right, rather than the redundancy of duty, since right is ambiguous in a way the duty is not. In addition we know that legal systems, such as those under Roman law, have existed without the concept of a right. To answer this puzzle about redundancy, we need to raise the question, what is the point of the concept of 'right' and the expression 'having a right against'? This is an important enquiry since it may tell us more about rights. In the ordinary case, in logic, we give the meaning of terms like 'right' by describing those conditions under which we apply the word in a true sentence. We saw how its application is connected with a process of argument. The truth conditions operate to spell out the conditions under which the term truly applies. But we know that we need sometimes to raise deeper questions about meaning. We may want to know why we draw the distinctions we do with right and duty and why we need the double description of a single relation. Some of these enquiries are crucial, for instance, when we seek to extend the range of an existing concept to new cases. How are we to tell whether we can or cannot plausibly extend the language of legal rights to animals unless we know what point is served by the concept under its existing applications?[7]

In considering the extensions of legal rights to new cases we draw upon our experience of right in the moral arena. Moral rights underpin legal rights in our arguments. Thus the point of the concept of right is in the area common to law and morality, and we need to bring together aspects which are separated in the logic of legal rights. In the case of rights correlative to duties, in addition, we need to understand why the description of a legal relation in terms of right is needed at all, since rights would seem to be redundant.

IV

The current, though tiny, literature on the point of the concept of a legal right seems to me to be defective in a number of ways. In that literature two ideas have been paraded to demonstrate why the language of legal rights is not redundant. In the first place, it has been argued that the notion of a legal right has a special role to play in the civil law, and that that role is not to be explained by the alternative language of duty alone, since the language of duty occurs in both the civil law and in the criminal law. That is Professor Hart's argument.[8] In the second place, it is argued that even if the concept of a legal right makes sense under the rules of the criminal law, nonetheless it is not redundant in law. It serves to show the respect accorded to individuals under legal rules, by allowing them to make claims, in a way that is not accommodated by ideas of duty. That is Professor Wasserstrom's argument.[9]

Hart argues that although rights necessarily entail duties, the converse does not hold. There are, he argues, general duties towards others under the criminal law that do not give rise to any corresponding rights. Under the criminal law no particular person or persons are intended to benefit from the rules imposing duties. The

---

[7] See M. Dummett, *Frege: Philosophy of Language* (London, 1973) at p. 413, for the idea of the *point* of our concepts. See M. Villey, *Leçons d'histoire de la philosophie du droit* (nouvelle édition, Paris, 1962), for the thesis that the concept of a right is absent in Roman Law.

[8] H. L. A. Hart, 'Bentham on Legal Rights', in *Oxford Essays in Jurisprudence*, second series, edited by A. W. B. Simpson (Oxford, 1973), pp. 171–201.

[9] R. Wasserstrom, 'Rights, Human Rights, and Racial Discrimination', *Journal of Philosophy* LXI (1964), pp. 628–41.

duties that exist in the civil law, however, exist by reason of the operation of special transactions, such as contracts, between particular persons. The point of the concept of a right is to be seen in the light of these special transactions in the civil law. In Hart's theory, what is emphasized is the special position of the person who has a legal right. Such a person has the choice whether a corresponding legal duty shall be performed or not. It is characteristic of right-conferring standards that under them the obligation to perform the corresponding duty is made to depend on the choice of the individual who has the right. As such a right-holder is more than a possible beneficiary of a duty.

The contrast with criminal law is made vivid. In the criminal law duties apply to persons who fall within the range of the general rules, without references to the choices of those who may be protected by the rules as to whether the duty shall operate or not.

It is consequently a mistake to argue that right and duty are everywhere interchangeable. The correlation between right and duty operates only in a single direction from right to duty. Hart concedes that if legal right and legal duty were everywhere interchangeable, then the concept of a legal right would be otiose. There is every reason to think that in such a case the acceptable theory of right would be a redundancy theory.

The difficulty with Hart's thesis is that there seem to be obvious counter-examples to it. Thus consider social welfare legislation which grants benefits and imposes duties upon officials in regard to the granting of benefits. It cannot be said here that the duties exist from some choice of any right-holder and yet it is as plausible here as anywhere to consider that claimants have rights. Hart recognizes this and weakens his theory of choice by saying that the beneficiary has the choice to sue or not to sue for his benefit. But if the theory of choice is weakened to the choice to *litigate* rather than to the *presence* of the corresponding duty, this leaves nothing in the theory to separate the civil from the criminal law. It is also true in the criminal law that there are choices to prosecute or not.

There are other difficulties about Hart's thesis. Thus there seem to be cases where lawyers ordinarily speak of rights under the civil law and yet there are no choices on the part of the right-holder. Infant beneficiaries under trusts have legal rights but they may be too young to be capable of a choice to sue. Only their guardians may have those choices. Hart argues that if the infant beneficiary were of full age he would have such a choice, and have it moreover without assignment from his guardian. But this conditional does not help Hart, for in the period while the infant is incapable of choice he is still the owner of a right. And surely infants have the right to a guardian—which right they would not have at full age. Here the appointment of a guardian is made by the court. In the same way we recognize that a lunatic has rights to visitors and to guardians. Any conditional here, in terms of what he could do if he were a sane adult, would turn a true proposition into a false one, since the lunatic would not have a right to a guardian if he were sane and could choose! What these cases show is that we can quite plausibly separate the beneficiary of any duty from the choice to initiate proceedings. There is no reason to think that we cannot conceive of some persons as the beneficiaries of duties, as right-holders, and yet allow the choice to initiate proceedings to some other persons. Thus we could make sense of legislation protecting persons where the choices to sue or not to sue rested with protective agencies or with special boards and not with the individuals. Nonetheless we think there are rights under such legislation in just the same way as rights in other relations. It would make no sense to have the institutions of duty here and nobody capable of instituting proceedings. Duties must be enforceable. But there is no reason to require, as Hart does, that the right-holder is the person who does the choosing to initiate proceedings. We can accept all kinds of vigilant agencies to exercise these sorts of choice, by actions they bring, to protect the legal rights of those not so capable.

Arguing in this way, we may feel that it makes just as much sense to talk of rights under the criminal law where duties are imposed as under the civil law.[10] The overriding difficulty is that although it makes just as much sense, we have not yet isolated what that sense is. So far the only theory keeping its head up is the redundancy theory for rights and its conclusion that the language of rights is matched by and made redundant by the language of duty.

Wasserstrom has argued that even if it is granted that rights correlative to duty do occur with as much sense under the criminal law as under the civil law, the redundancy theory nonetheless is not plausible. It would still be necessary to preserve the language of rights everywhere.

Wasserstrom argues that the point of the language of rights lies in the way it serves to reflect our ideas of being entitled to make claims upon others. Of course duties must be enforced, but the idea of having a right introduces a crucial perspective. Where persons can make claims upon others in the name of right, rather than in the name of privilege or of request, a legal system is recognizing valuable individual concerns. Thus where rights are claimed in respect of basic needs, the system is reflecting the recognition of a man's worth and this is not reflected by the corresponding language of duty. Imagine, argues Wasserstrom, a group of farmers from the southern states of America who, contrary to the general run, accept that they have duties in respect of their slaves regarding their health and welfare. The

[10] D. Lyon's conclusion in 'Rights, Claimants, and Beneficiaries', *American Philosophical Quarterly* VI (1969), pp. 173–85. I am indebted to this article.

farmers may describe their own situation only in terms of the presence
of duties to provide those services. If the language of right is missing
from their descriptions, then a crucial element is missing. The failure
to see and to describe corresponding rights in the negroes involves an
inability to conceptualize the negro as a person with standing to
protect his basic needs. In the absence of right, says Wasserstrom, the
failure of any duty will be just a matter of conscience and it reduces
everything to the level of privilege or request. But some things,
Wasserstrom continues, are not to be requested but rather are to be
claimed as a right. A conception of rights therefore means the
recognition of a sort of equality in law whereas a conception of duty
ignores this.

We all share a concern to expose the prejudices against which
Wasserstrom is inveighing, but the defects in his arguments cannot
pass. There is no reason to think that the distinctions between right
and privilege cannot be reflected in the alternative language of duty.
The crucial feature of the case is to see how the duties of the
southerners are described. If they are described as merely duties of
conscience or duties towards other white farmers then those duties are
of course inadequate. But no reference to the correlative right will
make them adequate. If, however, the services and protection some
southerners give their slaves are described by them as duties towards
the slaves, rather than as rights in the slaves, what is lost in this
alternative description? The answer to this cannot be that one sort of
description reduces the relation to privilege whereas the other does
not. This is just not true. Nor can the answer be that one sort of
language ignores the respect for men whereas the other sort of
language implies it. The farmers may well think that the language of
duty equally reflects their concern for others. On the other hand, I do
not see how a southerner contradicts himself, in grudgingly accepting
that his slaves have certain rights, and yet in not accepting them as his
equal.

What the example prompts is the question whether any valuable
features result from the description one way rather than another.
There is nothing in Wasserstrom's arguments to show that there is
anything more than a difference of perspective in the different
descriptions of a legal relation. This, at the end of the day, may be all
that can be said—that to convey a relation by reference to right is to
describe that relation from the point of view of the beneficiary rather
than from the point of view of the burdened person. So the difference
is a difference of style. No extra content is conveyed by the language of
right in place of the language of duty. In the same way we reflect a
different perspective when we describe a relation one way as 'X is the
parent of Y' and another way as 'Y is the child of X'.

There is little in this feature of style to recommend that we retain the language of right. If we were concerned to eliminate frills from legal theory, an investigation into the point of the concept of right is revealing. The conclusion is that we can completely account for any legal relation of protection by eliminating the language of right in favour of duty. If we capture in rights no more than the possible benefit from the presence of duty, then at the deeper level we might say that under legal systems these are really only relations of duty.

This was the conclusion that Bentham reached.[11] He accepted a redundancy theory of right. He conceded that there was unnecessary duplication for a single relation and argued therefore, that a rational code would be a code in which legal relations were described only by expressions of duty and penalty. Though right is an indispensable primitive in logical theory, it may be an unnecessary trapping at any deeper level than logic.

V Corrective justice

Logical analysis and the analysis of function are not the most important tasks of philosophies like jurisprudence and ethics which have practical problems. More important enquiries concern the analysis of justification and the way we make out a case for particular obligations and standards. To clarify what we mean when we assert, for instance, a duty to protect privacy, is not yet to have justified or established such a duty. When we attempt to make out a case, of course we need to establish the limits of various obligations; but clarification is not justification.

Moral philosophers who try seriously to justify rights tend to be anti-utilitarian. They often complain that utilitarians do not take rights seriously.[12] That complaint could mean no more than that utilitarians only take duties seriously, and it is worth remembering just how much social reform in the area of governmental and institutional obligations was achieved by utilitarians who took duties seriously.

The complaint, however, is recording something more than that utilitarians in their analyses of law ignore the language of rights. It is saying something about justification. In most versions of utilitarian ethics, all interests count in the same way, to be weighed at the end of the day in order to promote those interests which serve the general public welfare. The amount of general welfare and the amount of social progress count for more than questions of any distribution or of fair shares. So utilitarians do not take seriously fair shares or rights. Anti-

[11] J. Bentham, *A General View of a Complete Code of Laws*, chapter 19 in *Works*, edited by J. Bowring (11 vols, Edinburgh, 1843) III, p. 195.

[12] See R.M. Dworkin, 'Taking Rights Seriously' in *Oxford Essays in Jurisprudence, op. cit.*, pp. 202–27. See also J. Rawls, *A Theory of Justice* (Cambridge, Mass., 1971), especially §77 on 'The Basis of Equality'.

utilitarians tend to think that certain interests are too valuable to be weighed along with all the rest against public interest in this sort of process. Certain interests, individual interests, they reckon, ought not to have to yield to public interests. Some interests also have a value in their distribution and call for equality of distribution rather than concern with just amounts. These special individual interests are rights and rights weigh or count in this moral philosophy in a way that other interests do not. Thus rights do not submit before the national interest or before any economic or social progress. They are guaranteed against this sort of reversal.

Such arguments strike a responsive chord in law where many lawyers[13] feel, for instance, that legal remedies to restore the moral equilibrium should not be lost just because of their great economic cost or because their effects are socially inefficient or because of some doctrine of unreasonableness. They feel that victims should not remain uncompensated because the damage caused was not foreseeable or excessive. They feel too that nuisances should not be tolerated just because the costs of closing factories are very great. This is taking rights seriously. To champion rights to this extent may sometimes seem, to utilitarians, to be uncompromisingly blinkered. The national interest, after all, is no more than a sum of individual interests. Working out the economic costs of legal solutions may work to benefit everyone.[14] To bankrupt one person in order to compensate another may seem harsh and inefficient. Do not governments and institutions also have interests which sometimes count in the strong way that only individual interests are reckoned to?

Of course the special sorts of interests, that weigh more than ordinarily, may equally be reflected within the language of duties. But they are not reflected in duties by utilitarians. So the complaint that utilitarians do not take rights seriously is not a complaint now about their logical or other analyses of law, but a complaint about their moral philosophy.

In recent years the doctrine has been defended that a theory of rights reflects those individual interests connected with the respect men feel for each other and their shared sense of justice.[15] Ordinarily a moral equilibrium exists between men. That equilibrium may be upset by wrong doing or by the unequal distribution of goods. Where it is upset there are individual rights to restore the balance. The doctrine of rights is restricted in consequence to certain interests which reflect the shared sense of justice between men in their moral equilibrium. It is

---

[13] For example, G. P. Fletcher, 'Fairness and Utility in Tort Theory', *Harvard Law Review* LXXXV(1971–2), pp. 537–73.

[14] R. H. Coase, 'The Problem of Social Cost', *Journal of Law and Economics* III (1960), pp. 1–44.

[15] Rawls, *loc. cit.*

worth reflecting upon the future of that current doctrine about rights. It is certainly the doctrine of our time. There is hardly room for alternatives today.

The thesis about rights has two consequences which utilitarians would find unacceptable. The thesis denies rights to unequals. Our sense of shared justice is not shared for instance with the subnormal, nor with animals. Here there is no room for a theory about rights resting upon a shared conception of justice. They are 'outside the scope of a theory of justice'.[16] It means that in those cases interests do not count or weigh in quite the same way as other interests. Otherwise the thesis about rights would be empty. 'Kantianism for people, but not for animals' has quipped one critic.[17] The trouble with rights, crudely, is their all too human perspective. As such they are ill-adapted to non-human perspectives.

Many people, including utilitarians, think that the interests of animals, for instance, should count for more than they do, that they should count sometimes in the way that human interests count,[18] and that they are not outside the scope of a theory of justice. It may well be therefore, that a theory couched in terms of duty is the sort of theory that needs reflecting in a moral philosophy. So the rights thesis errs in its concern for a shared sense of justice and in ignoring non-human concerns.

Secondly, utilitarians feel that the promotion of values like happiness are beneficial irrespective of the way they are distributed.[19] In promoting this doctrine, they feel that any interest may sometimes be outweighed by benefits elsewhere, so that no interests specially count for more than others before final weighing. They reach this conclusion by denying what anti-utilitarians curiously accept, namely that national or social interests are something more than, or different from, a sum of individual interests. Utilitarians are reductionist about social or national interests. They argue that the welfare of a society consists only in the welfare of its members. Hence there is no hostility between individual and social interests as there is in the rights thesis. In concentrating upon social welfare in this reductionist way, utilitarians give less room to individual fair shares or rights and more room to collective interests. So they feel there is room for increasing benefits in amount whatever the distribution of the benefits. The

---

[16] Rawls, *op. cit.*, p, 512.

[17] R. Nozick, *Anarchy, State and Utopia* (Oxford, 1974), chapter 3, pp. 35–42.

[18] On animals' interests and utilitarian defences for them, see L. Tribe, 'Ways not to Think about Plastic Trees: New Foundations for Environment Law', *Yale Law Journal* LXXXVIII (1974), pp. 1315–48. H. J. McCloskey, 'Rights', *Philosophical Quarterly* XV (1965), pp. 115–27, denies that animals have interests. But do not animals have property and therefore interests?

[19] D. Parfit's point in 'Later Selves and Moral Principles' in *Philosophy and Personal Relations*, edited by A. Montefiore (London, 1975), pp. 137–69.

rights thesis is non-reductionist in a way that is difficult to understand. The marking off of individual interests there, for special concern, means that anti-utilitarians think of social interests or national interests as something over and above any sum of individual interests. It is not clear what sense is to be given to this.

It may be interesting to reflect that the future may well regenerate the language of duty in order to promote interests in areas where the rights thesis is prevented from promoting them.

Once again we meet here in the area of justification, as we met earlier in analysis, the thesis that we perhaps do not need the notion of rights to argue within and about legal theory.

VI

The thrust of this chapter has been that analysis operates at various levels in response to different problems. There is no single analysis of right. In logic there may be a local place for the notion of a right. There it may be regarded as an indispensable primitive in the logical theory underpinning legal systems. But that is limited progress to make. In deeper areas of legal theory the concept of a right may not aid understanding. In contemplating the point of our institutions there is a plausible thesis that the concept of a legal right is redundant. There it may be an unnecessary trapping. Equally, in the areas of practice where we justify our moral and legal positions, concentration upon rights may hinder reform and make fictions of interests like social interests.

At deeper levels than logic we might say that we make more progress towards understanding our legal concepts and practices by the language of duty than by the language of rights. We may think that philosophers should perhaps swim against the current now, and that in constructing theories in the face of this set of problems we should not take rights too seriously.

7

Individual rights against group rights

Nathan Glazer

I

The United States today is in the midst of a great national debate which must have bearing, in time, for any nation that is composed of many ethnic and racial strands—and that means the great majority of the nations of the world. The debate, which takes place in the executive, legislative and judicial branches of government, in the scholarly periodicals and the mass media, among unions and employers, in schools and universities, centres on the meaning of justice for minorities that have previously been treated unjustly. What it has done for us is to underline how simple were our understandings of the problems of racial and group discrimination in 1964, when one of the major pieces of legislation in American history, the Civil Rights Act of 1964, was passed. That Act, among other things, made discrimination in employment on the basis of colour, religion, sex, or national origin illegal, and made discrimination on the ground of race, colour, religion or national origin in the use of federal funds by any recipient of such funds illegal. Since almost all institutions are now recipients of federal funds, under one kind of programme or another, federal agencies may reach into and change the practices of schools, colleges, local government, state governments, universities, hospitals and many other institutions.

In 1964, in the United States, ending discrimination seemed a simple matter. Presumably one could recognize a discriminatory act—we don't hire blacks, or we don't promote them, or we don't pay them more than X dollars, or we don't allow them into this college or hospital. And one could devise penalties to punish such acts. Many cases are brought every day under the Civil Rights Act of 1964 and other pieces of legislation, federal and state, that ban discrimination, and many people who have been discriminated against find relief under these acts. The penalties are sufficiently severe—in particular, the granting of back pay for a period of years to individuals who have been discriminated against in employment—to make employers careful to avoid discrimination. The effects of the Act, it has been argued, were evident in a marked improvement in the numbers of blacks employed in better jobs after 1964.

Individuals take these actions to complain against discrimination, in order to vindicate rights that have been denied because of a group characteristic. Can we, however, solve the problems of group discrimination by using the language, and the law, of individual rights?

In that question is encapsulated the dilemma of justice for discriminated-against minorities. The individual has received discriminatory treatment because of a group characteristic. The law is written so as to vindicate the rights of individuals. But can the rights of individuals be vindicated, can the effects of past discrimination on the groups be overcome, if only that individual who takes action on the basis of discrimination receives satisfaction and compensation as the result of his individual charge of discrimination? Does not every other individual who is a member of the group also require satisfaction and compensation? But if the whole concept of legal rights has been developed in individual terms, how do we provide justice for the group? And if we provide justice for the group—let us say, a quota which determines that so many jobs must go to members of the group—then do we not, by that token, deprive individuals of other groups, not included among the discriminated-against groups, of the right to be treated and considered as individuals, independently of any group characteristic?

These are the issues that have arisen in the United States. I would like to break them down into a number of questions:

1   Why are our laws written as if the problem of discrimination is one of action against individuals; why do we in effect assert that justice in the face of discrimination is justice for the individual, rather than a new and equal status for the group?

2   Can laws and practices written as if the grievance is one borne by individuals overcome the effects of group discrimination and provide satisfaction to groups?

3   If, alternatively, we provide compensation to individuals on the basis of minority-group membership, have we deprived individuals of majority groups of rights?

4   Is there any general principle that can guide us as to when we should try to overcome discrimination by concentrating on the rights of individuals, and when we should try to overcome it by concentrating on the rights of groups?

Let me explain the perspective from which I will approach these questions. I am a sociologist, not a political philosopher or a lawyer. As a political philosopher or a lawyer, I would try to find basic principles of justice that can be defended and argued against all other principles. As a sociologist, I look at the concrete consequences, for concrete societies, of different policies. And here one major principle guides me. It is whether those practices lead to a general acceptance of the policies meant to overcome discrimination as good and decent policies, and lead to the widest measure of acceptance, among minorities as well as majorities. That may be denounced as a purely pragmatic or 'functionalist' principle, which leaves aside the great objectives of equality and justice. But these objectives are incorporated in that principle, too, because men today will not accept arrangements which maintain great inequalities and which offend strongly their sense of justice. These are key realities to be taken into account in using the pragmatic principle I have proposed: what policies to overcome discrimination give us the opportunity to best satisfy all the groups of a multi-ethnic society so they can live in some reasonable degree of harmony?

II

It is an interesting problem to ponder why it is that the deprivation of individual rights on the basis of some group characteristic—race, religion, national origin—is nevertheless treated, in law, at least in American law, as a problem of protecting the rights of an individual. The Fifth Amendment to the constitution, which limits the federal government and provides the language used in the Fourteenth Amendment, the foundation of constitutional protection for blacks and other minorities, reads: 'No *person* shall . . . be deprived of life, liberty, or property, without due process of law' (my italics). And the Fourteenth Amendment, adopted to protect the rights of the newly freed slaves, reads: 'No State shall make or enforce any law which shall abridge the privileges or immunities of *citizens* of the United States; nor shall any State deprive any *person* of life, liberty, or property, without due process of law; nor deny to any person within its jurisdiction the equal protection of the laws' (my italics). Citizens, persons—this is the language designed to defend a group, blacks, and which by extension of activist Supreme Courts defends the rights of Chinese, Japanese, Indians, Mexican-Americans, Puerto Ricans, aliens, women and many other groups defined in various ways. The same kind of language is to be found in the Civil Rights Act of 1964 and the Voting Rights Act of 1965; they refer to no single group. The legislation, just as the constitution, attempts to be colourblind in a society where colour and national origin are key realities determining in some measure the fate of the individuals of any group.

It is not only the constitutional and legal language which attempts to overcome the problems of group prejudice by guaranteeing the rights

D

of individuals; the most important American philosophical contribution to the problem of justice in recent times, John Rawls's *A Theory of Justice*, also ignores the problem of justice for groups, as Vernon Van Dyke points out in a perceptive essay. Van Dyke writes:

> He stipulates that those in the original situation 'should care about the well-being of some of those in the next generation' (p. 128), but he does not make a comparable stipulation about racial, linguistic, religious or national groups that are weak or disadvantaged or that cherish or want to preserve their distinctive characteristics and identity. . . . I do not see in the book a single reference to differences of language. Race is mentioned mainly to be ruled out as a ground of discrimination. Religion is mentioned at a number of points, but almost always with the individual believer in mind rather than the collective body of the faithful.[1]

It is an intriguing problem, and undoubtedly the answer is that the language and theory of the protection of human rights developed in a time and place (England in the seventeenth century) when the issue was seen as one of deprivation because of conscience, because of individual decision and action, rather than one of deprivation because of race, colour or national origin. England was relatively homogeneous, *except* for religion and political attitudes which largely flowed from religious conviction. These were seen as individual decisions, and to protect diversity was seen as an issue of protecting the diversity that flowed from individual decisions.

But what of that diversity that flows from the accidents of birth into a pre-existing community—defined by race, national origin, or religion? As Vernon Van Dyke reminds us, by pointing out that Rawls in speaking of religion has 'the individual believer in mind, rather than the collective body of the faithful', religion involves not only individual choice, but in the great majority of cases faith determined by birth, just as much as colour or mother tongue is determined by birth. This makes it very different from an act of individual conscience, as one can well see when one considers the meaning of Catholicism and Protestantism in Northern Ireland, of Islam and non-Islam in Malaysia. It would be play-acting in these countries to try to solve the serious problems of group conflict by legislating the freedom of the practice of religion, for that is not the issue. The issue in these countries, and in other countries where religious conflicts take on what I would call an ethnic character—that is, conflicts of groups of contrasting cultures defined by birth—is the relative economic and social positions of the two religious communities, not the free practice of religion.

[1] Vernon Van Dyke, 'Justice as Fairness: For Groups?', *American Political Science Review* LXIX (1975), pp. 607–14, at p. 607.

Is there an alternative legal and constitutional language to protect individuals who are penalized because of a group affiliation? Of course there is. It is the language that specifically guarantees the rights of groups, by name, that specifically reserves for groups a certain proportion of posts in government, in the civil services, in the universities, in business. This kind of approach to group rights is clearly just as compatible with a regime committed to human rights as the approach which focuses only on the individual. In one measure or another, we see this kind of approach in Canada, Belgium, India, Malaysia. Yet in the United States the attempt to reserve places, by number, in key areas of political life and economy is strongly resisted as a subversion of individual rights. And indeed, the revolutionary effort in the middle 1960s to establish a firm legislative basis for overcoming discrimination against blacks and other minorities expressly used language which protected the individual, carefully avoided specifying in any legislation what groups were to be protected, and specifically banned any approach which emphasized reserving places for different groups. This was the clear intention of Congress, and the American people, majority and minority, when the Civil Rights Act of 1964 was passed. To protect against the possibility that the Act might make possible a group remedy—let us say, quotas for employment for some groups that had been discriminated against—this was specifically forbidden in the Act. Perhaps that demonstrated the general naïveté that prevailed as to what would be necessary to raise a whole group that had faced discrimination over a long period of time. We have already pointed out that, in other nations, a different approach has been taken to the problem of raising a group—an approach that has straightforwardly adopted numerical quotas to ensure that appropriate numbers of the group received the benefits of education or employment. And so we have 'reservations' in India, and special programmes to increase the number of Malays in higher education and business employment in Malaysia.

As against this group-based approach, the American approach, both in legislation and in the important Supreme Court decisions that preceded and succeeded it, used the language of individual rights. It was in each case an individual that brought suit—*Brown* v. *The Board of Education*, *Griggs* v. *Duke Power*. One must neither overestimate nor underestimate the significance of the language and law that emphasize the vindication of an individual's rights. One must not overestimate it: it was organizations representing group interests that were sought out by individual plaintiffs, or that alternatively sought them out. It was the resources of groups that were required to argue cases up to the Supreme Court. It was the position of the entire group that one hoped to raise by individual test cases. If Brown could not be segregated on the basis of race, neither could White nor Wilkins nor any other black.

If Griggs could not be denied a job because the test he took for employment did not properly test his aptitude or capacities for the job in question, neither could any other black be denied employment on that basis.

But we should not underestimate either the significance of the individual aspect of these rights. Each case goes into the individual's account of discrimination, the damage to the individual. And even if the justices know well that by acting against an individual complaint of discrimination, they are raising the status and enhancing the rights of an entire group, it was expected—certainly in 1964—that these rights would become effective because *individuals* would claim them, and because they would now be treated as individuals, without distinctions of colour or national origin.

III

Could such an approach to overcoming group discrimination—the approach that assumed that individuals would act to vindicate their rights, and that the actions of individuals would overcome the deprived status of groups—really be effective? One of the main charges against the Civil Rights Act of 1964, as written and intended by the agencies that enforce it, is that it is unreasonable to expect that a group would overcome a heritage of generations of discrimination by the actions of *individuals* to acquire, on their own initiative, education, jobs, political representation. It was for this reason that the agencies involved began to take actions that aroused a good deal of dissent in Congress.

To begin with, they began to require that large employers take censuses of their employees on the basis of race and ethnic group, in order to make a preliminary assessment of whether certain groups were absent or underrepresented in certain levels of employment. Note that the first step in requiring these reports was to decide which groups an employer would have to report upon. The legislation was silent on which particular groups were protected from discrimination—all individuals were protected from discrimination on the basis of race, colour, national origin, religion. But in order to set up a system for employer reporting, some groups had to be selected, by administrative regulations, as being the particular focus of Congressional attention. It was a rather strange categorization of groups that the enforcing agency adopted for reporting. There was no question that negro Americans were the major concern of the Congress, as they were the major target of discrimination. Thus employers were required to report on the number of negro employees. Mexican-Americans and Puerto Ricans, two large groups of lower than average educational and occupational achievement, were incorporated into a new category of 'Spanish-Surnamed' or 'Hispanics', which also included anyone with a Spanish name, whether his or her origin was Spain or Cuba or some other place. Finally, a fourth category was defined, 'Oriental' or 'Asian American', which consisted principally of Chinese and Japanese. All the rest were 'others' or 'whites'. Educational agencies required reporting on the same categories from colleges and universities and schools.

The problem of the reporting system was, first, that it created amalgams by including groups that had presumably faced discrimination and those that had not (for example Mexican-Americans and Cubans); secondly, that it set up a category composed of groups (Chinese and Japanese) that had faced discrimination but had nevertheless already overcome the handicaps of discrimination to score higher in education and occupational achievement than the 'others' who were to serve as a benchmark by which to determine statistically the elimination of discrimination; thirdly, that it excluded some groups that felt they too, whether in the past or the present, had faced discrimination. Thus Americans of Italian, and Polish and other Slavic origin have often felt they have faced discrimination; but they were lumped with the 'others'. Jews have certainly faced discrimination but were also included among 'others'. In effect, the enforcing agencies had created two kinds of groups by this system of reporting—those that were its peculiar concern as objects of possible discrimination, and those that were of no concern at all and received no recognition as facing possible discrimination. A new form of the famous Orwellian principle was introduced: all groups were protected again discrimination according to the law, but some groups according to the enforcing agencies were more protected than others. Drawing a line between the first and the second was no easy matter in a complex multi-ethnic society where group prejudice has a long history and where it would be a foolhardy social analyst who would claim that only the four affected categories defined by the enforcing agencies were even today subject to discrimination.

A second problem arose with the reporting system: it was used to make presumptions of discrimination. While the law (the Supreme Court may now take the same position, but this is not clear) rejects the notion that statistical disparities may be evidence of discrimination, this in effect is how the agencies enforcing civil rights laws acted. They took statistical disparities as evidence of discrimination, and tried to pressure employers, public and private, into overcoming them by hiring on the basis of race, colour, and national origin—exactly what the original Civil Rights Act of 1964 had forbidden.

But was there any alternative to censuses of given groups and presumptions of discrimination on the basis of disparity? The defenders of this approach pointed out that to attack discrimination in any other way was costly to the individual who had faced discrimination and uncertain of satisfactory results. The individual would have to complain of discrimination to the enforcing agency, wait for investigation, conciliation, a final decision of whether his case was sound, possibly subsequent court proceedings. Or alternatively he would have to begin litigation on his own. And once having initiated a case, how was an enforcing agency or a court to settle the question of discrimination? Discriminatory acts could be rationalized away, concealed behind other ostensible bases of action, dissembled, would be difficult to determine precisely. It was easier to go to the numbers.

Was then the congress simply naïve in its assumption in 1964 that discrimination was not to be overcome by seeking disparities and imposing quotas? I think not. There were two important reasons why such an approach could be defended. The first was that in a democracy each group wields political power. That political power would in many cases prevent the bland hiding of discrimination behind rationalizations. With political power would come political representation and representation in the government service (where political considerations directly dictate appointments at the highest levels, and are influential at lower levels). Even without the warrant of specific law, political representation would lead to some rough justice in the distribution of government jobs, contracts and favours so that each group would get a share. Thus, in determining candidates for public office, parties often use as one principle the 'balanced ticket'— each major group is represented on the party list of candidates—for in a two-party system each party must appeal to almost every group. Representation in elected office means influence in making political appointments to government service. Political appointees in government service hand out contracts, place government money in banks, provide benefits of various types to businesses, universities, schools. In effect, political representation is seen as a key to more general representation of all the major segments of a society. And the Civil Rights Act of 1964, supplemented by an extremely severe Voting Rights Act of 1965, ensured that all obstacles to the registration and voting of minority groups would be swept away, as indeed they have been.

The second reason why Congress might well have believed that a purely individual approach to overcoming discrimination was not utopian was that other groups that had faced discrimination in the past—Jews, Chinese, Japanese—had, even without the powerful assistance of federal civil rights legislation, risen on the basis of individual initiative. If discrimination was illegal, if penalties for discrimination were, even if at only the margin, severe, would one not expect that the initiative of blacks, Mexican Americans, and Puerto Ricans would also operate to raise them politically, educationally, and economically?

Was this faith justified? It would be possible to answer that by studying intensively progress made by minorities in the five years between 1964, when the Civil Rights Act was passed, and 1970 and 1971, when policies based on requiring employment to reach statistical goals or quotas became increasingly common in the United States owing to the regulations of executive agencies and the rulings of federal courts. This is not the place for such an examination. Nor do we have fully satisfactory techniques to separate out, in any social change, one cause from a variety of others that are operating. It was after all also during those years that black demands were most militant and the fear of urban riots and possible urban insurrections greatest. Nevertheless, it is my judgement that great progress was made in those years, and that the point of view of Congress on minority progress was vindicated by that progress: black political representation did rapidly increase (it has continued to increase), black movement into colleges and universities leapt upward, black progress in closing the gap in earnings between whites and blacks was substantial.[2]

Of course this judgement is disputed; there is a great battle of the statistics and their interpretation which one cannot go into here. But behind the battle of the statistics lie ideological orientations. Those who feel American society is irredeemably racist, that the public opinion polls showing a decline in prejudice are simply deceptive, that black progress and progress for other minorities is impossible except on the basis of the most powerful governmental intervention, try to find in the statistics the evidence that supports their judgement of no or little progress. Those who believe that prejudice and discrimination have declined in the United States, that the United States is still basically an open society in which deprived groups and immigrants can achieve equality with older settlers and groups, see in the statistics the evidence that vindicates their faith.

Aside from this basic orientation, there is another difference in view that separates pessimists and optimists. Those who believe that the black has been severely damaged by centuries of slavery and discrimination and prejudice do not see how simply opening up non-discriminatory opportunity can raise the black (and one may, in lesser measure, make the same argument for other groups). Too many blacks are too crippled to act individually to take advantage of new non-discriminatory opportunity. And therefore one cannot count on

---

[2] See Nathan Glazer, *Affirmative Discrimination* (New York, 1976), pp. 40–43; Nathan Glazer, 'Affirmative Discrimination: Where Is It Going?', *International Journal of Comparative Sociology*, special issue edited by William Petersen (forthcoming); Richard Freeman, *Black Elite* (New York, 1977).

individual initiative, one must assure by goal and quota that given numbers of blacks are employed, promoted, taken into colleges and professional schools.

IV

This brings us to our third question. If we set a number, if we say one must employ one black teacher for one white teacher until the number of blacks reaches twenty per cent of the teaching force—as a judge in Boston requires—or if we say that sixteen per cent of all places to a medical school must be reserved for certain specified minorities—as the Medical School of the University of California at Davis has done—are we depriving the majority, the non-minority group, of any rights? Let me point out that the kind of action I have described is now widespread in the United States. Many police and fire departments must hire today on the basis of racial quotas, many teaching and supervisory appointments must be filled on this basis, many medical schools and other professional schools have adopted quotas. And a major constitutional case, which will be decided by the Supreme Court, will take up this issue. This is the case of Bakke, who applied for admission to the University of California Medical School, was denied admission twice, and claims his individual right to admission on a non-discriminatory basis was denied because the school reserved sixteen per cent of its places for minorities.

Is it a fair claim he makes? One can answer Bakke—and he has been so answered, in many *amicus* briefs filed with the Supreme Court—that very few of the many applicants to medical schools are accepted in any case; that blacks, who form eleven per cent of the population, have only two per cent of the doctors; that these numbers will not increase unless a specific effort to reach a certain number of black admissions is made; that one cannot argue that there is discrimination against the majority when they have eighty-four per cent of the places.

But on the other hand, it can be argued that the black proportion in medical schools has increased greatly in recent years; that there are other ways of recruiting blacks to medical schools than by setting a fixed numerical quota; and that the constitution and the civil rights laws forbid discrimination against any *person* on account of race, colour, or national origin, and this applies to whites, as well as blacks. Blacks were given the opportunity to enter the medical school both by means of the regular admission process, and by means of the special admission process for minorities, for which sixteen per cent of places were reserved. Whites were given the opportunity to enter the medical school only by means of the regular admission procedure. As a result, lesser qualified minority applicants were accepted in place of majority applicants.

If one thinks of a rough justice proportioned according to the size of groups, then Bakke loses. There are very few black doctors, there should be more. But if one thinks of individual rights, the right to be considered in one's own person independently of race, colour, national origin, Bakke wins.

There are two notions of justice in conflict here, one which says justice is apportioning rewards to groups on the basis of proportionality, the other which says justice is to be colour-blind, to consider only the individual. Bakke can say: 'I don't care how many black and white doctors there are, I want to be considered for admission on my individual merits, independently of race. *I* want to be a doctor; it is not the white race that wants another doctor.'

While it is an issue of admission to medical schools that has reached the Supreme Court, it is generally accepted that the principles governing employment and promotions are not very different. Here, too, one faces the same conflict: justice as proportionality by group or justice as the consideration of the isolated individual regardless of race, colour, national origin, religion.

The American people, raised on the language of individual rights, are remarkably uniform in their views. The Gallup poll recently set the following question: 'Some people say that to make up for past discrimination women and members of minority groups should be given preferential treatment in getting jobs and places in college. Others say that ability, as determined by test scores, should be the main consideration. Which point of view comes closest to how you feel on this matter?' More than eighty per cent of the respondents chose merit. Even among blacks, sixty-four per cent of the respondents chose merit. Individualism, one may say, is still strong in America.

It would be nice if one could avoid the dilemma, if individual choice in a multi-ethnic society, in the absence of discrimination, aggregated into a rough proportionality that meant justice satisfying both the individual and the group standard. But it doesn't—or it hasn't yet. That is the problem. Can one rest on principle when there are these substantial differences of representation between racial and ethnic groups? Or is it the task of a just society to make representation equal, even if this means the individual is not treated as an individual, but must be considered as a member of a group?

V

Is there a principle that suggests which course a multi-ethnic society will or should follow: whether to deal with discrimination and group difference by establishing numerically defined places in polity and economy for each group, or, alternatively, to emphasize the right of the individual to be considered without regard to group characteristics for election to office, for appointment to government posts, for employment, for admission to educational institutions? I have already placed in opposition to the dominant individual rights approach that we see in the United States and, I believe, in the United Kingdom, in France and in Australia, the approach in terms of rights for groups that we see, in different degrees, in Canada and Belgium, in Lebanon before its tragic civil war, in Malaysia and India. Undoubtedly if I knew more about other multi-ethnic states (for example Czechoslovakia and Yugoslavia) more could be added to the group approach. One may also add South Africa as a state committed to group rights—though the use of the term will certainly sound ironic here. The legitimation for the removal from politics and the higher reaches of the economy of blacks, coloured, Indians, is that each group is distinct and to be kept separate. This rationalization can be seized on by the subordinate groups to demand group representation at the centre.

Whether or not a nation elects to handle multi-ethnic diversity by formally ignoring it or by formally recognizing it has no bearing on whether it is a democracy or not: whether it be a democracy, a 'people's democracy', a dictatorship, or an autocracy, either approach to multi-ethnic diversity is possible. What this suggests to us is that the *form* of response to diversity, individual rights or group rights, should have no bearing on whether we consider that nation responsive to human rights and to civil rights. Rather, we should realize, there are two quite distinct forms of response. In the United States, divided as we are by this issue, we seem to believe that one course upholds the constitution while the other betrays it, and thus that one course enhances democracy and equality in the United States but that the other course reduces it. While I am a partisan of the individual rights approach for the United States, aware as I am of the diversity in handling these kinds of issues in other equally democratic countries of the world, I cannot see that the issue can be decided in these terms.

I believe the key principle, that does in fact and should determine for a multi-ethnic state—including the United States—whether it elects the path of group rights or individual rights, is whether it sees the different groups as remaining permanent and distinct constituents of a federated society or whether it sees these groups as ideally integrating into, eventually assimilating into, a common society. If the state sets before itself the model that group membership is purely private, a shifting matter of personal choice and degree, something that may be weakened and dissolved in time as other identities take over, then to place an emphasis on group rights is to hamper this development, to change the course of the society, to make a statement to all its individuals and groups that people derive rights not only from a general citizenship but from another kind of citizenship within a group. And just as laws and regulations are required to determine who is a citizen of the state and may exercise the rights of a citizen, so would laws and regulations be required to determine who is a citizen of a subsidiary group, and who may exercise the rights of such a citizenship.

If, on the other hand, the model a society has for itself, today and in the future, is that it is a confederation of groups, that group membership is central and permanent and that the divisions between groups are such that it is unrealistic or unjust to envisage these group identities weakening in time to be replaced by a common citizenship, then it must take the path of determining what the rights of each group shall be. Thus, Canada sees itself a federation of two founding peoples, English and French; Malaysia cannot conceive of the dividing line between Malay and Chinese disappearing; Belgium tried to work as unitary state, with the dominance of the French-speaking element, but once the Flemish-speaking element asserted its claim to equal rights, its constitution had to accept these two central elements in the state as permanent.

There are of course other important differences among multi-ethnic states: there are those in which one group was clearly subordinate, a minority facing discrimination; and there are those in which different groups did not see each other as arranged in a hierarchy of higher and lower. But in almost all multi-ethnic situations groups do rank each other. While the hierarchy may not be as absolute as it is in South Africa, or as it was in the southern United States, that is, a strict caste-like situation fixed in law, there is generally some sense of grievance by one group against another. But this issue does not affect the principle I have proposed. Groups that are roughly parallel in political and economic strength may nevertheless be so diverse, or consider themselves so different, that the idea of integration or assimilation to a common norm is inconceivable. This is certainly the case for Anglophones and Francophones in Canada, Flemish-speakers or French-speakers in Belgium. On the other hand, groups that are ordered in a hierarchy, that are considered 'higher' or 'lower', reflecting real and substantial economic and political inferiority, may nevertheless set as their ideal and ultimately expect integration into the common society. This was certainly the objective of the American negro civil rights movements until the late 1960s—black leadership (then called negro leadership) wanted nothing more than to be Americans, full Americans, with the rights of all other Americans. And this was also the objective of European immigrant groups to the United States, many of whom as immigrant and second-generation communities faced discrimination. Similarly, West Indian immigrants to Britain viewed themselves and, I believe, still view themselves as black Britons, wanting nothing more than full acceptance, the same rights in all spheres that all other citizens hold.

There is thus such a thing as a state ideology, a national consensus, that shapes and determines what attitude immigrant and minority groups will take toward the alternative possibilities of group maintenance and group rights on the one hand, or individual integration and individual rights on the other. It is interesting to contrast immigrant groups, from the same background, to Canada and the United States. Canada, because it was already based on two founding, distinct national elements, gave more opportunity for incoming minority groups to select group maintenance as a possibility. Thus it appears there is somewhat less integration, somewhat greater commitment to group maintenance, among Slavic groups and Jews who went to Canada, compared with the same groups when they went to the United States. The United States, whatever the realities of discrimination and segregation, had as a national ideal a unitary and new ethnic identity, that of American. The United States was a federation of states which were defined politically, not ethnically; Canada was a federation of peoples, organized into different provinces. The impact of this originating frame for ethnic self-image can be seen on subsequent immigrants into the two countries. And, I would hazard, one can see the same difference in legal institutions, with a greater willingness in Canada formally and legally to accept the existence of ethnic groups. I would not exaggerate the difference, but it is there.

But what I would emphasize is that for some societies a choice is possible. There are facts and ideals that point both ways. And now I return to the United States. The society can go one way or the other, toward individual rights or group rights—which is why the division over the Bakke case is so intense, even among those elite, educated elements of the society that in the 1960s, during the civil rights struggle, formed a solid phalanx of one opinion in favour of individual rights. In the United States, coexisting with the facts of eager immigrant groups entering the country, becoming Americanized, rising economically, socially, politically, were the equally powerful facts that the status of blacks, of Chinese, of Japanese, of Indians was defined in law, in racial terms, for purposes of discrimination and segregation. And coexisting with the over-arching national goal or image of one nation, of individuals endowed with equal rights, was a minority sentiment—encouraged undoubtedly in part by discrimination—in favour of cultural pluralism, the maintenance of group identity. A large body of opinion in the United States always fought discrimination and segregation as a betrayal of the American ideals of individual rights and equality. In the middle 1960s, with the passage of the Civil Rights Act of 1964 and the passage of the Immigration Act of 1965, which eliminated all references to race and all quotas on the basis of nationality, it seemed as if the individual rights ideal had triumphed. But then, as we saw, the question came up of how to achieve practical equality, and we began to slide again toward group definition, this time for purposes of correction and benefit, rather than for purposes of discrimination and segregation.

Clearly one key issue is whether previously subordinated or separate groups can envisage progress under a course of individual rights. Gordon P. Means puts the issue well. He writes:

> A good case can be made both for and against group special privileges. Such a system can be an effective strategy for inducing rapid social change, in settings where cultural variables need to be taken into account. Without preferential privileges, there may be no inducement for improving the opportunity structures of deprived or encapsulated cultural and ethnic groups. Where group identity and communal and ethnic prejudices permeate a society, it is naive, if not hypocritical to talk about the equality of opportunity based upon individual achievement and universalistic norms.[3]

I would emphasize the words, 'where group identity and communal and ethnic prejudices permeate a society'. If in a society the groups are sharply divided from each other, so that their boundaries are clear, are firmly set by law or custom, are not expected to become permeable and if they live in a long historical tradition in which group identification has been used and is used for purposes of discrimination and separation, there may be no alternative: special preferences are necessary to protect the inferior group and for inter-group harmony. Thus one must determine an issue of fact. But one must also determine an issue of direction. Because if inferiority and difference are being overcome, one must consider the negative consequences of selecting the path of group rights and preferences, and one would wish to avoid them if one can. As Means continues: 'Yet, when all has been said, it must also be acknowledged that the system of group special rights does involve considerable social costs and is a rather crude strategy for inducing social transformation.'

An Indian Supreme Court justice has also suggested to us language helpful in confronting the dilemma. The case before him dealt with special preferences which were originally granted to the most backward castes, but which—a tendency one might expect in the case of special preferences—have become more expansive to include other less backward castes and classes. Justice Krishna Iyer of the Indian Supreme Court wrote:

---

[3] Gordon P. Means, 'Human Rights and the Rights of Ethnic Groups—A Commentary' in *International Studies Notes* 1 (1974), pp. 12–18, at 17.

The social disparity must be so grim and substantial as to serve as a basis for benign discrimination. If we search for such a class, we cannot find any large segment other than the scheduled castes and scheduled tribes. Any other caste, securing exemption from [the appropriate constitutional guarantee of 'equal opportunity'] by exerting political pressure or other influence, will run the risk of unconstitutional discrimination.[4]

This is a test we can apply. Is the social disparity so grim and substantial that there is no alternative to benign discrimination?

We now understand the basis, in facts and ideals, which will move a multi-ethnic society in one direction or another. But what are the implications of choosing one path or another? If we choose the group rights approach we say that the differences between some groups are so great that they cannot achieve satisfaction on the basis of individual rights. We say, too, that—whether we want to or not—we will permanently section the society into ethnic groups by law. Even if advocates of group rights claim this is a temporary solution to problems of inequality, as they do in India and in the United States, it is inconceivable to me that benefits given in law on the basis of group membership will not strengthen groups, will not make necessary the policing of their boundaries, and will not become permanent in a democratic society, where benefits once given cannot be withdrawn. In effect, American society, which had moved toward an emphasis on individual rights in which group affiliation and difference was to become a matter of indifference to the state, concerned only that such affiliation did not affect the fate of the individuals, would become something very different if it continues to move along the path of group rights. More groups will join the four already selected as special beneficiaries. And for every movement in the direction of group rights, the individual's claim to be considered only as an individual, regardless of race, colour or national origin, would be reduced, as more and more places were reserved to be filled on the basis of group affiiliation.

When a society, such as American society, faces both ways, with one tradition insisting on a unitary identity, and another—a minority tradition—arguing for cultural pluralism, with many groups barely differentiated from each other in wealth and power, but others lagging much further behind, there is no escape from the problem of difficult choices. Are the differences between groups in American society 'so grim and substantial' that there is no other course but special privilege? To me, and to other analysts of the American scene, the speed with which gaps between blacks and whites—and gaps between

[4] Robert L. Hardgrave Jr, 'DeFunis and Dorairajan: "Protective Discrimination" in the United States and India', unpublished paper delivered at the 1976 annual meeting of the American Political Science Association, Chicago, Illinois, 2–5 September 1976.

most minority groups and the rest of the society—are being closed in political representation, in income, in education, is rapid and satisfactory. To others, these changes are dismissed as paltry and insignificant. To me, too, the overall direction of American society has been to a society with a common identity, based on common ideals, one in which group identities are respected as private and individual choices but in which these identities are strictly excluded from a formal, legal, constitutional role in the polity. To others, the fact that groups were in the past legally defined for purposes of discrimination and segregation and exclusion is sufficient reason why we should resurrect the same and new legal group definitions for purposes of reparation and compensation.

The choices we are now making on the difficult issue of individual rights versus group rights will tell us which view of American society will prevail, and what, in consequence, the fate of individual rights in American society is to be.

8

Marxism, socialism and human rights

Alice Erh-Soon Tay

I

'Human rights', Professor Hermann Klenner of the German Democratic Republic told the recent Australian World Congress of the International Association for Philosophy of Law and Social Philosophy,

> are neither eternal truths nor supreme values. . . . They are not valid everywhere nor for an unlimited time. They are rooted neither in the conscience of the individual nor in a God's plan of creation. They are of earthly origin . . . a comparatively late product of the history of human society—and their implementation does not lie in everybody's interest. In their essentials, man's interests are not the same everywhere and they cannot even be the same in any particular country under the conditions of the system of private ownership of the means of production.[1]

Nevertheless, human rights are for Professor Klenner and for Marxists generally of profound historical importance, battle-cries for social change that helped to create the modern world. Even in their eighteenth-century Jeffersonian formulation as rights of liberty and equality they helped not only to bring down the *ancien régime* in France, but to usher in the Democratic Republic of Vietnam, whose declaration of independence in 1945 referred to the claim in the American Declaration of Independence that 'All men are created equal.' Fidel Castro, defending himself in court in 1953, sought to legitimise his revolt by referring to the birthright of man as set out in the American and French declarations; the Black Panther Party in its 1966 manifesto included a lengthy excerpt from the American Declaration of Independence. Thus, while Professor Klenner

[1] Hermann Klenner, 'Human Rights: A Battle-Cry for Social Change or a Challenge to Philosophy of Law?', paper circulated to participants in the World Congress on Philosophy of Law and Social Philosophy, Sydney/Canberra, August 1977, pp. 8–9.

emphasizes that bourgeois rights by themselves cannot point to the non-bourgeois future, that they must be amended and given new economic and social content, and that they are, in his view dishonestly, now being used as a weapon in the Cold War, he does insist that Marx did not treat law as a 'negligible' factor and human rights as simply one of the bourgeois illusions. Marx's concern was to actualize and concretize human freedom and he thus paved the way for a scientific conception of human rights.

There is no doubt that Marx saw in what he called the bourgeois revolution and its associated proclamation of the rights of man and the citizen initially, at a specific historic stage, an immense step forward for mankind, a crucial liberation from the bondage of feudalism. But it was only, for him, a partial liberation—a political emancipation of man which was also an emancipation of civil society, of greed and acquisitiveness, of the social power of property, of the possibilities of new kinds of economic enslavement. The bourgeoisie had wrought not only a political liberation, but an incredible revolution in human power and capacities, in the means of production and their effectiveness, in man's capacity to subject nature to his needs and to escape from rural idiocy and dependence on natural forces. The further progress of mankind required a new, social revolution—the abolition of the right of private property and its conversion into a social function, the abolition of wage-labour and the division of labour, the transcending of what Marx called 'the narrow horizons of bourgeois right' based on the inherent conflict of man with man, in the 'truly human community of communism' in which each would give according to his capacities and receive according to his needs, in which the whole concept of abstract, individual rights and duties would be overcome.

In the thought of Marx and in socialism generally, therefore, there is a certain fundamental ambivalence, direct and implied, on the question of human rights. Socialists did see that early declarations of rights, as Dr Kleinig put it earlier in this volume, 'were regarded as justifications for revolution and other acts of political violence'. They *were* crucial battle-cries in the emergence of modern republicanism, democracy, universal suffrage, the abolition of feudal distinctions and disabilities, the downfall of autocracies. While socialists believed that as socialists they were concerned with a subsequent stage of history— the gradual or revolutionary transformation of capitalism into a socialist community—socialist parties in fact, in the nineteenth century and in many places in the twentieth, have been fighting not an advanced industrial capitalism but the survivals of the old order or the emergence of new, 'fascist' and military, autocracies. Much of the cutting edge of the Communist Manifesto was directed not against capitalism, but against traditional societies, medieval superstition, feudalism and despotism. Even today, the greatest successes of communism have been in societies in which such traditional social and political arrangements were especially strong or in those colonial and semi-colonial societies in which the struggle for political independence, for national liberation, was relevant and strong. Marx spent as much of his time supporting meetings for the liberation of Poland as he spent organizing or supporting strikes; the radical socialist today spends as much time speaking of South Africa, Chile, Angola, Indonesia and China as he spends on the problems of the working class in modern industrial societies. The language and the values of the eighteenth-century declarations of rights therefore have continuing appeal for the socialist and for those concerned with these issues. What socialists call the bourgeois revolution is not yet consummated throughout the world; socialists and communists are doing, or pretending to do, much of its work and naturally appropriate many of its slogans. These slogans, indeed, for much of the world are still the symbols of progress, of modernity, of human liberation. Hence, even the communist states make much use of the words 'democracy' and 'democratic'; hence their constitutions, whether they mean it or not, proclaim at least some of the traditional rights of man and the citizen.

At the same time, socialists and Marxists do stand, and have always stood, in a fundamentally critical relation to the bourgeois revolution and above all to its elevation of the right of property—property which in the course of the nineteenth century increasingly became property in the means of production, distribution and exchange, property that meant power over others. The productive work and economic life of society, they insisted and insist, must be brought under rational, public control, whether by planned centralized administration or decentralized community control. In either case, the right of private property as anything but the right to property for personal consumption and use had to be abolished or most severely restricted. Since the eighteenth-century rights of man quickly became, in the second half of the nineteenth-century, what socialists saw as reactionary, counter-revolutionary battle-cries *against* state or community interference and control, since they were entrenched in many places in constitutions that acted as impediments to state action, let alone nationalization and socialization, socialists came to be increasingly critical in the economic and political sphere, and often in the cultural, of the elevation of the individual and his rights altogether. The Soviet legal theorist, E. B. Pashukanis, correctly expressed one strong historic strain in socialist thinking when he insisted that bourgeois law, with its concentration on the individual and its reduction of everything to relations between legal personalities, must be replaced by plan and the use, as a substitute for civil and criminal law respectively, of the concepts of social harm and social danger. The Soviet educational theorist, A. S. Makarenko, expressed an allied and similarly strong strain in socialist thinking when he wrote that, in the socialist society

> There should be no isolated individual, either protruding in the shape of a pimple or ground into dust on the roadway, but a member of a socialist collective. . . . The individual personality assumes a new position in the educational process—it is not the object of educational influence, but its carrier. It becomes its subject, but it becomes its subject only by expressing the interests of the entire collective.[2]

Coupled with the insistence that individuals were social and historical products, that there were, as Marx had said, no unhistorical human nature in general and no asocial or pre-social individual, this strain in socialist thinking cut savagely into the philosophical and the ideological proclamation of abstract human rights preceding social arrangements and capable of acting as courts of appeal against such arrangements. The socialist court of appeal, for much of the history of socialism, was the public welfare, or the needs of the working class, or the demands of the collective or of history. The individual was something whose nature socialism would fundamentally alter.

Tactically and politically, socialists could and did, in the light of historical circumstances and of their own position in the socialist spectrum, emphasize one or other of these attitudes to the rights of man and the citizen, always excluding from them, if speaking favourably, the sacred right of property. Generally, socialists have emphasized their positive relation to the classical rights of man and the citizen in their struggle against autocracies and attacked the abstract elevation of these rights in their relationship with their own citizens. The process of de-Stalinization in the Soviet Union, the re-emergence of intellectual dissent in communist countries and the rise of Western Marxism, often drawing on a socialist humanist interpretation of Marx and a Western commitment to democracy in politics, together with a worldwide trend, stemming from allied war aims and proclamations in the second world war, toward the elevation of human rights and freedom, have put pressure on socialists and communists to define more fully their position on human rights, both in morals and in law. Democratic socialist parties continue, as in the past, to be eclectic, to draw on and hold in loose and undefined relationship a number of social traditions—the elevation of the individual and his rights, especially of freedom and equality, the application of criteria of social utility and 'rational' use of resources, and an emphasis on the preconditions of universal 'welfare' and equality, the individual's

---

[2] As translated in Eugene Kamenka, *Marxism and Ethics* (London, 1969), p. 58, from A. S. Makarenko, *Sochineniya* (7 vols, Moscow, 1950–52), V, p. 333 and II, p. 403.

'right' to receive benefits from the community and the state unrelated, at least directly, to his contribution or effort. In Marxism, which strives toward a greater theoretical coherence in these matters, the following position on human rights is emerging:

1   The underlying ethic and goal of Marxism is socialist humanism— the creation of the fully developed, unalienated, free and conscious individual, who will find in a socialist society that his natural relations with other individuals are those of free and spontaneous cooperation and who, in that benevolent social framework, will seek fully to develop all his capacities and potentialities.

2   While the ethical and legal systems of past periods of class societies, including the elaborations of doctrines of human rights, show signs of their origin in specific class societies and both in their content and function serve class interests, they also contain general human elements and recognition, however limited and distorted, of the rules necessary for any human community whatever and of the dignity and rights to which human beings, as human beings, are entitled.

3   Such rights and rules, however, cannot be treated simply in the abstract. In particular, the political sphere cannot be divorced from the social and economic. Rights must not be seen as freedoms from but as freedoms to, and as such they require constant attention to the economic and social setting in which men live and, in societies of private property and class conflict, total reorganization.

The conflict between more and less 'democratic' wings within Marxism, and more generally within socialism, lies in the extent to which the emphasis is placed on paragraphs 1 and 2 or on paragraph 3, in the precise interpretation of paragraphs 1 and 2 and in the extent to which the importance of human rights is stressed *within* the movement, even while it is seeking to achieve or consolidate its power.

The tension over human rights and a certain ambivalence toward them are not confined to the attitudes of communist countries and socialist parties. Contemporary developments in the west reveal a similar ambivalence or vacillation over the rights of the individual. The vacillation is between emphasizing freedom as autonomy, freedom 'of', and demanding the preconditions for 'freedom' to live on a minimal standard, freedom as guaranteed security. This is the distinction implied but obscured in the 'Four Freedoms' (freedom *of* speech and expression, freedom *of* worship, freedom *from* want and freedom *from* fear) proclaimed by President Roosevelt in 1941. On the one hand, there is in the present age a remarkable elevation of the individual and his rights, seen as classical rights to freedom from coercion, manipulation, discrimination. They have been extended not only to servants, Asians, Africans and 'coloured' and 'primitive' peoples generally, but to women, children, and by some to animals and plants. On the other hand, the attempt to give social and economic content to the concept of equality, the demand for rational control and egalitarian distribution of resources, the new concern with environment, ecology, urban planning and husbanding of resources have all led not only to an enormous extension in the power of the state and the demands for its assistance, but to a deliberate and conscious depreciation of the individual and his claim to autonomy. 'Doing one's own thing' may be in fashion; but only as long as it is doing one kind of thing and not another. The tension, of course, is most easily resolved if one's own thing is doing nothing at all.

II

Theory is one thing, practice another. The Stalin constitution of 1936 formally guaranteed certain basic freedoms—freedom of speech and assembly, freedom of the press and the right to demonstrate, the inviolability of the person, of his home and of his correspondence, the independence of the judiciary, open and public trials, the right to defence counsel, freedom of conscience and of religious worship (though not of religious propaganda, which was and is interpreted to include the religious education of minors).

It is now admitted by everyone except the Chinese and Albanian Stalinists that the Stalin constitution and the wartime Soviet national anthem with its claim that there is no other land so free were a hollow mockery of Soviet conditions, that the repressions and purges that accompanied Stalin's rule went far beyond anything that could be justified by the exigencies of revolutionary transformation or the need to preserve and maintain socialism in the face of foreign and internal hostility, and that they were based on sustained and systematic disregard of law and any respect for human dignity or human rights. The facts were brought out by Soviet leaders themselves, notably in the revelations at the 20th and 22nd congresses of the CPSU in 1956 and 1961, though they are now again being soft-pedalled. We now know that Stalin killed more Russians than the Germans did, that whole nationalities, of which the Chechens and the Volga Germans are the most notable examples and the Crimean Tatars another, were virtually exterminated through forced population transfers and the severest of camp conditions. It is conceded by Soviet sources that roughly one tenth of the population of a Stalinist labour camp died each year from undernourishment, exposure and overwork; most prisoners were sentenced to periods ranging from ten to twenty-five years. Yugoslav sources estimate that twenty million people or over one tenth of the then population of Russia perished in Soviet labour camps or before Soviet firing squads in the period of Stalin's rule. Some five million of these died during the forced collectivization of the peasants. There are still those, both in the West and in the Soviet Union, who want to forget or gloss over these facts, who cavil whether the figure was really twenty million or only fifteen million, who want to notice only the Russian soldiers and civilians killed by the German invaders and who never mention the thousands of Russian soldiers executed for an indiscreet letter home or for having been unwise enough to escape from German imprisonment in order to rejoin the Soviet forces. We can now read about all this in the illegal and semi-legal literature of the most respected of Soviet writers—in Solzhenitzyn's *One Day in the Life of Ivan Denisovich*, *Cancer Ward*, *The First Circle* and *The Gulag Archipelago*, in Evgenia Ginzburg's *Into the Whirlwind* and, more guardedly, in the heavily censored writings of Paustovsky and Ehrenburg, not to speak of the countless letters from political prisoners and former political prisoners that now find their way abroad. As Robert Conquest shows in great detail in his *The Great Terror*, the writings of Soviet authors now confirm fully and in surprisingly interlocking detail the worst horror stories in all the books of the 'I was the victim of the GPU' variety. They show up as the product of cynical lying or fantastic gullibility almost any story about the Soviet Union between 1930 and 1953 that was not full of horror. Besides the holocaust that Stalin let loose upon some 200 million people from Riga to Vladivostok, the doings of Franco and the Greek junta were a joke. In the twentieth century only the Nazis have matched and exceeded the scale, brutality and sustained organization of the Stalinist terror and its cynical disregard of its own laws.

Was all this, as Soviet leaders claim, simply an unfortunate historical accident, the consequence of nothing but the cult of the personality of Stalin, the product of the paranoia and suspicion of a Georgian dictator who misused a system geared to freedom and happiness? Are the present milder but still individually severe repressions simply hangovers from Stalin's technique of government, carried on by a generation trained in his style? Did the rot—the use of what Russians euphemistically call 'inadmissible methods'—really begin only when Stalin turned the secret police against his own colleagues and the membership of the Communist Party? Did it not go back at least a few years earlier to the brutal collectivization of the peasants, which launched Stalin on the path of government taken earlier by Ivan the Terrible? What are we to make of 1918, when Lenin and Trotsky suppressed and brutally butchered the Kronstadt sailors, the heroes of the revolution, who were now demanding genuine elected soviets and the cessation of any use of censorship and the CHEKA against fellow socialists and revolutionaries?

A revolution, says Mao, is not a dinner party; a wrong cannot be righted without exceeding the proper limits. The English, who attained to the same profound wisdom without benefit of the Little Red Book, say you cannot make omelettes without breaking eggs. The history of the Soviet Union, however, suggests there is somewhat more at stake than this. The rejection of a state based on law and of a society based on the presumption of individual rights and liberties goes very deep in the Soviet system and in much Marxist theory and practice. This is the ultimate explanation of the failure of the Stalin constitution to become any kind of safeguard for civil rights, and of the still unhappy situation, the powerlessness and rightlessness, of dissenters in all communist states.

The new draft constitution of the USSR, approved for widespread popular discussion by the Presidium of the Supreme Soviet on 3 June 1977, in its chapter 7 on 'The Basic Rights, Freedoms and Duties of Citizens of the USSR', extends slightly the range of civil liberties and human rights 'guaranteed' (but never protected) by the Stalin constitution, primarily in the direction of extending and concretizing economic 'rights' (that is benefits) in line with the increasing prosperity of the Soviet Union. It augments the right to work with a right to choose a profession or type of occupation and employment in conformity with the vocation, abilities, professional training and education of the citizen and with due reference to the needs of society. It also guarantees a right to health and old-age care, compulsory universal secondary education and housing and formulates more carefully the political rights and freedoms of citizens, including the rights to participate in the conduct of state and social affairs and to make suggestions and criticisms to government organs. But it is careful to maintain the Marxist tradition of linking individual rights with the performance of social duties and to spell out clearly the limitations on these rights. As in the Stalin constitution, the most important civil rights and freedoms (speech, assembly, street demonstrations, religious worship and privacy) are granted only to be exercised 'in conformity with the interests of the working people and for the purpose of strengthening the socialist system'. In the new draft constitution, these and other rights are also to be 'inseparable from the performance by citizens of their duties'. While there are significant differences of detail in the new constitutions promulgated in most East European countries in the late 1960s and early 1970s, they contain much the same guarantees of civil liberties on condition that they are not used against the socialist system, much the same linking of rights and duties and much the same emphasis on guaranteed benefits as economic 'rights'. Even the People's Republic of China, with its much greater degree of overt politicization of law and administration, its rejection of the Soviet concept of socialist legality and its decision not to promulgate general codes of law, listed in its constitutions, both before and after the Great Proletarian Cultural Revolution, the conventional civil liberties guaranteed to citizens—equality before the law, the right to vote without reference to nationality, race, sex, occupation, social origin, religious belief, education, property status and length of residence (unless deprived of such right by law), freedom of speech, assembly, association, procession and demonstration, freedom of the press and of religious belief (but not of propaganda), inviolability of the person and home, privacy of correspondence, freedom of residence and change of residence and freedom to engage in scientific research and other cultural pursuits—while putting on the citizen the duty to 'abide by the Constitution and the law, uphold discipline at work, keep public order, respect social ethics', protect public property, pay taxes and perform military service according to law. But above all, as article 26 of the new constitution adopted on 17 January 1975 puts it: 'The fundamental rights and duties of citizens are to support the leadership of the Communist Party of China, support the socialist system and abide by the Constitution and the laws of the People's Republic of China.' The implications of that, in China and in all communist states, go very far indeed. Most, perhaps—if we exclude Cambodia—almost all, communist states have abandoned the mass terror of Stalinist days, but their rulers have remained tough autocrats, allowing just so much liberty and no more, using their secret police and their enormous social, economic and administrative powers to ensure that there shall be no public, politically significant, dissent, that individual rights will indeed be subordinate to social duties, to duties to the state.[3]

[3] [The draft Soviet constitution of 1977 discussed above was promulgated into law in October 1977 with only slight modifications—none of which affect the preceding characterization and discussion of the Soviet position. News reports from the People's Republic of China in December 1977 suggest that a third constitution, replacing that enacted in 1975 and approaching more closely a concept of Socialist legality, may now be under—cautious—consideration. A.E.S.T. January 1978.]

9

Human rights and international law

J. G. Starke

Nothing is more untrustworthy than general impressions or general assumptions not based on precise knowledge. This proposition applies with particular force to the subject of the protection of human rights under international law. On the one hand, there is the lingering impression or assumption that before the movement during the second world war which led to provisions concerning human rights being included in the United Nations Charter of 26 June 1945, there was little or no recognition by international lawyers of the need for protecting the fundamental rights of human beings by norms of international law. On the other hand, there is the prevailing current supposition that developments since the adoption of the United Nations Charter have resulted in a complete body of general or universal norms of international law binding all member states of the international community to protect human rights, that is to say, human rights of the kind proclaimed, for example in the Universal Declaration of Human Rights adopted by the General Assembly of the United Nations in December 1948. The truth is that while many persons have been beguiled by one or both of such beliefs, neither is correct.

Well before the United Nations Charter of 1945 one can find in the writings of a number of nineteenth-century international lawyers[1] the notion that there are certain fundamental rights of mankind, not of course specifically described as 'human rights', which ought to come within the scope of rules of international law guaranteeing their sanctity. The word 'ought' requires emphasis, for it was only in certain limited directions that the practice of states, let alone rules of international law, reflected this view. There were instances, in the nineteenth century, of humanitarian intervention by the great powers

---

[1] See, for example, J. C. Bluntschli, *Das moderne Völkerrecht der civilisierten Staaten als Rechtsbuch dargestellt*, 3 Auflage (Nördlingen, 1878), pp. 360–63, 370.

to prevent persecution or infliction of cruelties[2]. Although it was dubious whether there was a right under international law so to intervene upon humanitarian grounds, the recourse to such intervention was nevertheless indicative of a limited international recognition of the need to protect certain human rights. Other particular isolated illustrations of such recognition, frequently mentioned in the standard textbooks of international law, were the Treaty of Berlin of 1878 under which the great powers exacted a pledge from Bulgaria, Montenegro, Serbia, Romania and Turkey to grant freedom of worship to their nationals and the various anti-slavery treaties or treaty provisions of the nineteenth century, culminating in the next century in the Geneva Slavery Convention of 1926 by which the parties undertook to suppress and prevent the slave trade, and the Supplementary Geneva Convention of 1956 for Abolishing Slavery, the Slave Trade, and Institutions and Practices Similar to Slavery.

Apart from other considerations, two theories or attitudes stood in the way of any general recognition by international law in the nineteenth century and first two decades of the twentieth century, of the need to protect human rights. First, there was the so-called 'dualist' theory, according to which only states were the subjects of international law. Individuals, on this theory, were objects but not subjects of international law, and without standing to enforce their rights before, or be heard by, an international tribunal.[3] Accordingly, this theory precluded the recognition at international law of individual human rights. Secondly, there was the doctrine that a state has complete sovereignty over its own nationals to the extent that such sovereignty constitutes a sphere of reserved jurisdiction into which international law is not permitted to reach.[4] This doctrine represented an obstacle to the concept of international protection of human rights, a concept which necessarily involves each state accepting a restriction of its sovereignty in becoming bound by external obligations not to deny protection to the human rights of its own nationals.

After the first world war, there were some more significant examples of the recognition, on the one hand, by international lawyers, and on

[2] See L. Oppenheim, *International Law*, 8th edn (London, 1955) 1, pp. 312–13. Professor Ermacora has described humanitarian intervention as 'a means of human rights protection', International Law Association, *Report of the 55th Conference, New York, 1972*, edited by L. D. M. Nelson (London, 1974), at p. 609.

[3] See H. Triepel, *Völkerrecht und Landesrecht* (Leipzig, 1899) *passim*, and cf. Sir H. Lauterpacht, 'The Subjects of the Law of Nations', *Law Quarterly Review* LXIII (1947), pp. 438–60 and LXIV (1948), pp. 97–119.

[4] Cf. J. L. Brierly, *The Law of Nations*, 6th edition by Sir H. Waldock (Oxford, 1963), at p. 291: 'Under customary law no rule was clearer than that a state's treatment of its own nationals is a matter exclusively within the jurisdiction of that state, i.e. is not controlled or regulated by international law.'

the other hand, by treaty practice and the practice of states, of the necessity for protecting human rights by international norms. As to international lawyers, there was the notable Declaration of the International Rights of Man adopted by the Institut de Droit International at its 1929 meeting,[5] the preamble to which recited that 'the juridical conscience of the civilized world demands the recognition for the individual of rights preserved from all infringement on the part of the State', and article 1 of which proclaimed that 'it is the duty of every state to recognize the equal right of every individual to life, liberty and property, and to accord to all within its territory the full and entire protection of this right, without distinction as to nationality, sex, race, language or religion.' The same concern was echoed in the individual writings of a number of international lawyers during this period.[6] As to treaty practice and the practice of states, reference may be made to the following:

1 the various clauses in the treaties made by the principal allied and associated powers with certain Central European and East European States after the first world war for the protection of the rights and welfare of racial, religious, and linguistic minorities;[7]

2 Part XIII of the Treaty of Versailles of 1919 (which has now become the constitution of the International Labour Organization), providing for the establishment of the International Labour Organization,[8] the purposes of which were, *inter alia*, to promote better standards of working conditions for men and women and their material well-being, and to uphold the freedom of association of employees—an important human right in itself;[9]

3 the references in article 22 of the League of Nations Covenant (part of the Treaty of Versailles of 1919), an article dealing with the mandates of former German and Turkish colonies and territories, to the 'principle' that the 'well-being and development' of the peoples of these mandated dependencies should form 'a sacred trust of civilization', and to the mandatory power's obligation to 'guarantee freedom of conscience and religion';[10]

4 the recognition during the first world war peace treaty negotiations of the right of self-determination[11], one of the most important human

[5] Institute of International Law, *Annuaire* XXXV (1929), pp. 289–300.

[6] See, for example, Hans Wehberg in *Friedenswarte* XXIX (1929), pp. 354–7.

[7] See C. A. Macartney, *National States and National Minorities* (London, 1934); Julius Stone, *International Guarantees of Minority Rights: Procedure of the Council of the League of Nations in Theory and Practice* (London, 1932).

[8] See G. N. Barnes, *History of the International Labour Office* (London, 1926) and C. W. Jenks, *Human Rights and International Labour Standards* (London, 1960).

[9] See C. W. Jenks, *The International Protection of Trade Union Freedom* (London, 1957), *passim*.

[10] Cf. H. Duncan Hall, *Mandates, Dependencies and Trusteeship* (London, 1948).

[11] See Sir A. E. Zimmern, *The League of Nations and the Rule of Law, 1918–1935* (London, 1936), pp. 199, 226.

rights, specifically recognized now by both the International Covenant on Economic, Social and Cultural Rights of 1966 and the International Covenant on Civil and Political Rights of 1966 (see below and p. 123); 5 the Geneva Slavery Convention of 1926, referred to above.

These examples are by no means exhaustive, but they sufficiently illustrate the point that it is a misapprehension to regard the international protection of human rights as unknown to international lawyers or to diplomatic negotiators before the outbreak of the second world war in 1939.

The second misconception referred to, the impression that there is a complete and comprehensive body of rules for the protection of human rights which is now firmly a part and parcel of international law rather than being largely norms *de lege ferenda*, is sufficiently disposed of by reference to the present state of ratification and acceptance of the two covenants mentioned above, which contain binding pledges by the parties to observe and respect the human rights therein dealt with. These two covenants, the International Covenant on Economic, Social and Cultural Rights of 1966 and the International Covenant on Civil and Political Rights of 1966 are at present, after more than ten years, binding on little more than a quarter, if that, of the states of the world. Both covenants, it is true, came into force in 1976, the former at the commencement of the year, and the latter on 23 March 1976 after being in each case ratified by a thirty-fifth state, thirty-five ratifications or acceptances being necessary for such entry into force. This means no more than that each covenant is binding as between the thirty-five parties concerned *inter se*, but not on those states which have so far abstained from ratifying or accepting the convenants. These non-party states may conceivably regard each covenant as containing a body of model guidelines or *desiderata*, but they are nonetheless not bound in international law to observe them. Covenants which are not obligatory on three quarters of the states of the world cannot be deemed to form a part of general international law.

It is worth remembering also that, at their highest, both covenants were planned as only the second stage of a programme designed to achieve an international bill of rights, based upon universally binding obligations of states, and reinforced by effective curial and administrative machinery. When such a programme was completed, it was conceived that the international bill of rights would represent an important component of general international law. Chronologically, the three stages were to be:

1 A general declaratory instrument defining the various human rights which ought to be respected; this was accomplished with the adoption by the United Nations General Assembly in December 1948 of the Universal Declaration of Human Rights.

2 A series of binding covenants on the part of states to respect such

rights as defined; this was in part achieved when in December 1966 the General Assembly of the United Nations adopted the two international covenants on, respectively, economic, social and cultural rights, and civil and political rights.

3 Measures and machinery for implementation of the covenants were to constitute the third and final stage. In the absence of the completion of the last stage, the projected international bill of rights remains more a promise than an achievement.

It may be urged that the protection of human rights has gone far, at least in the European region with the European Convention for the Protection of Human Rights and Fundamental Freedoms signed by the member states of the Council of Europe at Rome in November 1950, and the supplementary protocols thereto, and in the American region with the Inter-American Convention on Human Rights, opened for signature on 22 November 1969. These regional sets of norms of international law, however, still fall short of constituting general norms of international law, even if we leave aside the procedural and jurisdictional weaknesses in the operation of the protective machinery provided for under the two regional conventions. Furthermore, a number of significant human rights are not the subject of protection, however feeble, under any binding international convention, whether general or regional.

It must therefore be accepted that, in the international law domain, there is no complete body of generally recognized rules for the protection of human rights, and that, with certain specific exceptions, such comprehensive general protection is largely in the *de lege ferenda* phase of development.

If regard be paid to the nature of the original impetus behind the movement for protecting human rights in the period 1941–5, leading to the human rights provisions in the United Nations Charter, it may not be a matter for surprise that, even thirty years after the adoption of that Charter in 1945, the protection of human rights is not comprehensively covered by general rules of international law. In that important period, 1941–5, during the second world war, it was not asserted that international law, as then constituted, protected human rights, but rather that international law *ought* to protect these rights. Thus in a lecture at Chatham House, London, on 27 May 1941, Hersch Lauterpacht, a noted protagonist of human rights and one of the most eminent international lawyers of his generation, stated only: 'The protection of human personality and of its fundamental rights is the *ultimate purpose* of all law, national and international.'[12] Later, in

---

[12] Sir H. Lauterpacht, *International Law: being the Collected Papers of H. Lauterpacht*, edited by E. Lauterpacht, 11 (Cambridge, 1975), at p. 47. These *Collected Papers* are in progress and appearing at long intervals.

the face of opposition from other eminent international jurists, he sought to read into the provisions as to human rights in the United Nations Charter and into the terms of the Universal Declaration of Human Rights of 1948 commitments in an international law sense which were not there,[13] thus proving that, before both instruments were adopted, human rights were not protected by general rules of international law.

The impetus for the protection of human rights in the period 1941–5 was essentially of a political nature. Its rationale drew strength from the conviction that since the second world war was due to the conduct of totalitarian states and since those states had trampled upon human rights, one important safeguard against the outbreak of war and for the preservation of peace was the protection of human rights. This was reflected in various 'war aims' declarations of the period, in which, incidentally the expression 'human rights' received its first emphasis at the official level. Thus in his notable message to Congress of 6 January 1941 President Roosevelt, making a call for the upholding of the 'Four Freedoms' ('four essential human freedoms') declared: 'Freedom means the supremacy of human rights everywhere. Our support goes to those who struggle to gain those rights or keep them.'[14] In the same year, in August 1941 on the occasion of the announcement of the so-called 'Atlantic Charter',[15] President Roosevelt and the British prime minister, Mr Churchill, subscribed jointly to a number of declarations, one of which was that they hoped to see established a peace which would afford to all nations the means of dwelling in safety within their own boundaries, and which would afford assurance that all men in all lands might live out their lives in freedom from fear and want. The expression 'human rights' occurred again in the joint declaration of the United Nations at Washington on New Year's Day 1942, in which it was proclaimed 'that complete victory . . . is essential to defend life, liberty, independence and religious freedom and to preserve human rights and justice.'

The goal of a post-war future in which human rights would be respected was again stressed in the year 1944, notably in the International Labour Organization's Declaration of Philadelphia, later

---

[13] Sir H. Lauterpacht, *International Law and Human Rights* (London, 1950), pp. 145–54.

[14] US Congress, House Documents, 77th Congress, document 1, 6 January 1941. The four freedoms were: 1) the freedom of speech and expression; 2) the freedom of worship; 3) the freedom from want; 4) the freedom from fear.

[15] See Julius Stone, *The Atlantic Charter: New Worlds for Old* (Sydney, 1943; reprinted 1945 with a new introduction), *passim*. On the connection between peace and human rights, see also K. Tanaka, 'Some Observations on Peace, Law and Human Rights' in W. Friedmann *et. al.*, editors, *Transnational Law in a Changing Society: Essays in Honour of Philip C. Jessup* (New York and London, 1972), pp. 242–56.

incorporated in the constitution of the organization.[16] That declaration looked to the attainment of conditions in which 'all human beings, irrespective of race, creed or sex, have the right to pursue both their material well-being and their spiritual development in conditions of freedom and dignity, of economic security and equal opportunity'. There was a more specific reference to 'human rights' and to 'fundamental freedoms' in the Dumbarton Oaks proposals of 1944, embodying a tentative scheme for a general international organization[17] which, together with the Yalta voting formula, formed the basis of the discussions at the San Francisco Conference of April to June 1945, which drew up the United National Charter. The proposed organization was to 'facilitate solutions of international, economic, social and other humanitarian problems and promote respect for human rights and fundamental freedoms'.

Further confirmation of the peace-oriented objectives involved in the promotion of respect for human rights is supplied by the very text of the United Nations Charter. Nowhere in the Charter is it stated or even implied that the aim is to produce a complete body of international law protective of human rights; the realization of human rights is to be produced at the national level by international cooperation. This, it is submitted, appears clearly from the text of article 13 of the Charter, where it is provided that the General Assembly is to initiate studies and make recommendations for the purpose of:

1 promoting international cooperation in the political field and *encouraging the progressive development of international law and its modification*;

2 promoting international cooperation in the economic, social, cultural, educational, and health fields, and assisting in the realization of human rights and fundamental freedom for all without distinction as to race, sex, language or religion.

If it had been intended that 'the progressive development of international law' should have extended to include the protection of human rights, this surely could have been stated in this key article of the Charter. There is additional confirmation elsewhere in this

[16] See C. W. Jenks, 'The Revision of the Constitution of the International Labour Organization', *British Yearbook of International Law*, XXIII (1946), pp. 303–17, and cf. N. Valticos, 'Normes de l'Organisation internationale du Travail en matière de protection des droits de l'homme', *Revue des droits de l'homme* IV (1971), pp. 691–771.

[17] Previous United States drafts of the Charter of the proposed organization had referred to 'human rights'; for example, the draft bill of rights of 1942, referring to 'a common programme of human rights', and a draft of August 1943, proposing the annexure of a 'Declaration of Human Rights'; see L. B. Sohn and T. Buergenthal, *International Protection of Human Rights* (Indianapolis, 1973), pp. 507–8.

instrument. In the preamble, the peoples of the United Nations 'reaffirm faith in fundamental human rights' and article 1 contains a redraft of the Dumbarton Oaks formula of 1944 in its formulation of the third 'purpose' of the United Nations as being 'to achieve international cooperation in solving international problems of an economic, social, cultural, or humanitarian character, and in promoting and encouraging respect for human rights and for fundamental freedoms for all without distinction as to race, sex, language, or religion'. This aim is repeated in article 55, where it is stated that the United Nations is to promote universal respect for, and observance of, human rights and fundamental freedoms 'with a view to the creation of conditions of stability and well-being which are necessary for peaceful and friendly relations among nations', while by article 56 member states '*pledge* themselves' to act jointly and separately for the achievement of these purposes.

Throughout the Charter, respect for and observance of human rights are stated in terms of general aims, purposes, and objectives, rather than expressed as imposing specific obligations on member states of the United Nations to protect specific rights (see for example, article 76 as to the trusteeship system). Nor is there any precise definition anywhere in the Charter of the content of these rights, although one particular right, that of self-determination, is referred to in articles 1 and 55, and underlies the provisions of chapters XI and XII as to non-self-governing territories and as to trust territories. Lauterpacht sought to draw wider inferences, disputed by other international lawyers. He argued that although the provisions of the Charter were imperfect from the point of view of enforcement, they constituted legal obligations of the member states and of the organization as a whole.[18] With all respect for so great a lawyer, this view is untenable, and it certainly has not commanded general support from the majority of governments of member states. Lauterpacht's view is also scarcely consistent with the fact that in the course of the discussions at the San Francisco Conference which drew up the United Nations Charter, certain proposals by the delegations of participating governments to impose upon member states specific legal obligations to respect human rights were rejected in favour of the present drafting.

Some writers have sought to derive from the advisory opinion of the International Court of Justice in 1971 on the Legal Consequences for States of the Continued Presence of South Africa in Namibia (South West Africa) support for the theory that the Charter does impose legal obligations in the field of human rights. They point to the passage in which the Court condemned South Africa's denial of human rights to

<hr/>

[18] Lauterpacht, *International Law and Human Rights*, op. cit., pp. 145–54.

the population of South West Africa in its capacity as a former mandatory power under article 22 of the League of Nations Covenant. The relevant dictum of the Court was that 'to establish . . . and to enforce, distinctions, exclusions, restrictions and limitations exclusively based on grounds of race, colour, descent or national or ethnic origin which constitute a denial of fundamental human rights is a flagrant violation of the Purposes and Principles of the Charter'.[19] It is maintained that the Court could not have employed the words 'flagrant violation' unless it conceived that the Charter imposed legal obligations.[20] However, this view, it is submitted, puts a gloss on the actual words used by the Court; the Court did not refer to a flagrant violation of legal obligations imposed on member states of the United Nations, but to a flagrant violation of the 'Purposes' and 'Principles' of the Charter, which are set out in articles 1 and 2 of that instrument, and in those two articles there is nothing in terms imposing a specific legal obligation to observe human rights.

In determining the relevance of the United Nations Charter for the protection of human rights under international law, one is on firmer ground in drawing attention to three points, namely:

1 Dealing with the subject of human rights in an international instrument of almost universal application has removed the question of the protection of human rights from the sphere of the reserved jurisdiction of a state over its own nationals and made it a matter of international concern—indeed a matter for legitimate concern of the United Nations and its competent organs, as will appear also from the second and third points.

2 Article 62 of the Charter provides in paragraph 2 that the Economic and Social Council of the United Nations may make recommendations for the purpose of promoting respect for, and observance of, human rights and fundamental freedoms for all. Apart from other considerations, this power given to the Economic and Social Council opened the way for the development of United Nations practices in the field of human rights, which by a normal process of evolution could lead to the emergence of customary rules of international law in that field.

3 Article 68 empowers the Economic and Social Council to set up a commission for the promotion of human rights and, as will be seen, the Human Rights Commission established by the Council and subject to Council directives has proved to be a cornerstone of United Nations activities and machinery for the protection of human rights.

The thirty-three years since the adoption of the United Nations

[19] International Court of Justice, *Reports of Judgments* (1971), pp. 16–345 at p. 57.
[20] Egon Schwelb in International Law Association, *Report of the 55th Conference*, at p. 585.

E

Charter have not seen the emergence of a complete and comprehensive body of rules of international law as to human rights; but there has nevertheless been a process of accumulation, in a somewhat unsystematic manner, of declarations, treaty provisions, court decisions, and practices, all concerned with rules or standards as to human rights. They represent only partial steps along the path towards a complete code of rules of international law on human rights. A schematic analysis of them is out of the question. All that can be attempted is a brief description of each in turn—a method of examination that must necessarily result in an incomplete treatment.

A convenient starting point is the Universal Declaration of Human Rights, adopted by the United Nations General Assembly in December 1948. This declaration could not and did not purport to be more than a manifesto, defining in detail a large number of human rights—not, of course, defined in the United Nations Charter—so as to provide in a solemn form a generally acceptable catalogue of the most essential inalienable rights of human beings. To reproach the Declaration for not providing the machinery of enforcement or implementation, or to criticize the fact that the Declaration is not in the form of a binding legal instrument, imposing specific obligations on the governments represented in the General Assembly which adopted it, is to misconstrue its original limited purpose. It was intended as a first stage, to be followed by a second stage of binding human rights covenants, and later by the final stage of methods and machinery for implementation.

Professor Gerald Draper has well described the Universal Declaration of Human Rights as 'a transitional instrument somewhere between a legal and a moral ordering',[21] and in that form and that sense it has had a remarkable influence on legal developments, at both the international and domestic levels. Numerous subsequent resolutions of the General Assembly of the United Nations have drawn on the Declaration as a code or standard of conduct,[22] it paved the way for the two international human rights covenants of 1966 mentioned above, and in one way or another contributed towards the conclusion of a number of important international conventions, including, for example, the convention of 1951 on the status of refugees, of 1953 on the political rights of women, of 1954 relating to the status of stateless persons, and the UNESCO convention of 1960 against discrimination in education. To that extent the Declaration has served well one of its

[21] G. I. A. D. Draper, 'Human Rights and the Law of War', *Virginia Journal of International Law* XII (1971–2), pp. 326–42 at p. 336.

[22] See John Carey, *UN Protection of Civil and Political Rights* (Syracuse, N.Y., 1970), appendix A, pp. 177–87, containing an excerpt from the United Nations Secretariat study, 'Measures taken within the United Nations in the Field of Human Rights', for a detailed examination of the influence of the Universal Declaration of Human Rights on law and practice, at both the international and domestic levels.

original purposes as a path-finding instrument. As pointed out in an official United Nations document:[23]

> During the years since its adoption the Declaration has come, through its influence in a variety of contexts, to have a marked impact on the pattern and content of international law and to acquire a status extending beyond that originally intended for it. In general, two elements may be distinguished in this process—first, the use of the Declaration as a yardstick by which to measure the content and standard of observance of human rights; and, second, the reaffirmation of the Declaration and its provisions in a series of other instruments. These two elements, often to be found combined, have caused the Declaration to gain a cumulative and pervasive effect.

Leaving aside the Universal Declaration of Human Rights, and its influence, various organs of the United Nations, the General Assembly, the Economic and Social Council, and the Human Rights Commission have contributed to the body of law and practice concerning human rights. The General Assembly on 14 December 1960 adopted the Declaration on the Granting of Independence to Colonial Countries and Peoples which, together with the appointment by the Assembly under a later 1961 resolution of a special committee to implement the Declaration, has done much to give substance to the right of self-determination. The General Assembly on 21 December 1965 adopted the International Convention on the Elimination of All Forms of Racial Discrimination, which came into force in January 1969, and which is widely considered to be the most effective of all international instruments concerning human rights; under the Convention there was established a committee on the elimination of racial discrimination with various innovatory procedural functions, and, through the medium of periodic reports from countries parties to the Convention, empowered to exercise a supervisory role in relation to the implementation of the Convention.

As to the Human Rights Commission, its most important contribution to date has been the basic work in the preparation of the drafts of the International Covenants of 1966 on, respectively, Economic, Social and Cultural Rights, and on Civil and Political Rights. However these covenants only came into force in 1976, when in each case the required number of thirty-five ratifications or acceptances was obtained (see also above p. 116). In the practical and procedural work of protecting human rights, the Commission has been only moderately successful. During the first two decades of its existence the Commission was not unfairly criticized for its

[23] United Nations Document A/CN. 4/245, 23 April 1971, at p. 196: Survey of International Law, a working paper prepared by the Secretary-General of the United Nations for the International Law Commission.

ineffectiveness: in 1947 it initially adopted the position that it had no power to take action on petitions or communications, received by the United Nations, complaining of the infringement of human rights. This was confirmed by a resolution, number 75(v) of 1947, of the Economic and Social Council, holding that the Commission was not entitled to take action upon individual human rights complaints. The solution was then adopted of the United Nations Secretariat observing a procedure of preparing for the Commission two summaries—(i) a non-confidential summary of communications or petitions dealing with principles of human rights; and (ii) a confidential summary of other communications concerning human rights, such summary to embrace individual complaints of breaches of human rights, the complainant's name not being recorded unless he consented to this.[24] Such a restricted view of the Commission's powers was widely criticized. Lauterpacht, for example, maintained that the Commission was not only entitled to take such action, but bound to do so under the terms of the Charter, and he urged that the right of petition in human rights cases was implied in the United Nations Charter as the very minimum means of safeguarding human rights.[25]

The situation changed in 1967 when the Economic and Social Council by resolution number 1235 authorized the Human Rights Commission to make, 'in appropriate cases and after careful consideration of the information . . . made available to it', a thorough study of situations 'which reveal a consistent pattern of violation of human rights', thus leaving unaffected individual complaints not revealing such a pattern of violation. In 1970, the Council authorized the Commission's Sub-Commission on prevention of Discrimination and protection of Minorities (established by the Commission in 1947) to follow the procedure of appointing a working group to review human rights petitions or communications received by the United Nations, so that the working group could bring to the attention of the Sub-Commission those petitions or communications (together with the replies of governments, if any) which appeared to reveal a consistent pattern of gross and reliably attested violations of human rights and fundamental freedoms. In 1971, after much discussion, the Sub-Commission adopted, at the request of the Economic and Social Council, rules and procedures for determining the admissibility of petitions or communications. The Sub-Commission has exercised its powers, but, as viewed by objective observers, the effective performance of its functions has been bedevilled by the two major difficulties of availability of time, and of difficulties in investigating the surrounding facts as to complaints.

Professor Malvina Guggenheim rightly said of the new system

---

[24] Carey, *op. cit.*, p. 145.

[25] Lauterpacht, *International Law and Human Rights*, *op. cit.*, at p. 230 and p. 244.

adopted by the Human Rights Commission in 1967–71 that it constituted 'a momentous step forward', and that 'for the first time in history an international body with almost worldwide membership has been given authority to consider complaints by individuals, groups or organizations, charging a state with human rights violations.'[26] While this is true, performance counts more than promise. The working group method is commendable, and was continuously used, in 1975–6, for example, in relation to the complaints of violations of human rights in Chile. It is only right to point out also that the Human Rights Commission has, throughout its existence, had recourse to a wide range of expedients, including fact-finding, negotiation, conciliation, provision of publicity, dissemination of information, education, and the inspiration of national legislative measures. According to one learned writer:

> The most effective methods for enhancing and protecting human rights, employing tools already used as well as those which might soon be accepted, would include investigation and negotiation, followed where necessary by publicity, and in *extreme cases* by impartial judicial procedures including criminal charges under established law. The non-coercive tools of aid to victims of oppression and education of national leaders should be continued [my italics].[27]

The impression remains, nevertheless, that despite the accumulation of declarations, resolutions, rules, standards, and guidelines within the framework of the United Nations, the abiding weakness is that of implementation, and at the same time politics may cut across the functions of promotion of human rights cast upon the Economic and Social Council and the Human Rights Commission by the Charter. One experienced observer has said: 'In the absence of an alert international public opinion, the record of the United Nations in the matter of implementation will continue to be one of frustration and lost opportunities, and governments will continue to manoeuvre pretty much as they like and so prevent the effective development of any machinery which might expose them to criticism.'[28] A more pungent criticism is that by a reviewer of a recent book on the proposals for a United Nations high commissioner for human rights: 'The protection and promotion of human rights by the United Nations

---

[26] Malvina H. Guggenheim, 'Key Provisions of the New United Nations Rules Dealing with Human Rights Petitions', *New York University Journal of International Law and Politics* VI (1973), pp. 427–46 at p. 427.

[27] Carey, *op. cit.*, p. 173.

[28] John P. Humphrey, 'The International Law of Human Rights in the Middle Twentieth Century' in M. Bos, editor, *The Present State of International Law and Other Essays* (Deventer, 1973), pp. 75–105 at p. 95. See also R. Cassin, 'La Commission des Droits de l'Homme de l'ONU, 1947–1971' in *Miscellanea W. J. Ganshof van der Meersch* (Brussels, 1972) I, pp. 397–433.

since December 10 1948 has been characterized by indecision, mistrust and delay.'[29]

Aside from the United Nations, the International Labour Organization (ILO) has received praise for its special implementation procedures in the domain of those human rights which are of special concern to it, notably the right of freedom of association. That right was given more formal and more detailed expression in two ILO conventions, the Convention of 1948 on Freedom of Association and Protection of the Right to Organize, and the Right to Organize and Collective Bargaining Convention of 1949. Special investigatory and supervisory machinery was established to examine alleged infringements of the freedom of association.[30] Complaints may be lodged against states whether or not they have ratified the conventions of 1948 and 1949; in other words, allegations may be examined even in the absence of a binding obligation upon the state in question to observe the terms of the conventions. The complaints are considered by the ILO governing body's Committee on Freedom of Association, composed of three government, three employee, and three worker representatives, a committee originally set up in 1951. Intractable cases may be referred to a fact-finding and conciliation commission. The work of the Committee on Freedom of Association may interact with the supervisory work of the ILO Committee of Experts on the Application of Conventions and Recommendations, for if the former committee draws attention to any default of performance by a member state of the ILO in respect to the 1948 or 1949 Convention, this will be closely examined by the Committee of Experts, and the government concerned will be asked to indicate further developments in its subsequent reports.[31] The Organization claims that during the period 1951–71 more than seven hundred complaints were examined by the Committee on Freedom of Association, in many cases with 'positive results'.[32]

On the question of implementation, reference may be made to the differences in the machinery set up under the International Covenant on Civil and Political Rights and that established under the International Covenant on Economic, Social and Cultural Rights. The former covenant provides for a committee with the responsibility of

[29] Ralph Beddard reviewing R. S. Clark, *A United Nations High Commissioner for Human Rights* (The Hague, 1972) in *International and Comparative Law Quarterly* XXIII (1974), p. 674. 10 December 1948 was the date of adoption and proclamation of the Universal Declaration of Human Rights by the General Assembly of the United Nations.

[30] See Jenks, *The International Protection of Trade Union Freedom, op. cit., passim*, and E. A. Landy, *The Effectiveness of International Supervision: Thirty Years of ILO Experience* (London, 1966), pp. 176–7.

[31] Landy, *op. cit.*, p. 177.

[32] 'Human Rights: is International Action Effective?' in *ILO Information* IX (1973), p. 6.

considering reports from states parties, and of addressing comments, if necessary, to those states and to the Economic and Social Council of the United Nations (see article 40). In the case of the latter covenant, however, in as much as it was felt that economic, social and cultural rights could be achieved less quickly than civil and political rights, because the latter rights could be safeguarded by immediate legislation, whereas the former rights depended upon resources becoming progressively available to each state, provision was made merely for the submission of periodical reports to the Economic and Social Council upon the progress made and upon the measures taken to advance the rights concerned.

The most important regional instrument dealing with human rights is the European Convention for the Protection of Human Rights and Fundamental Freedoms signed by the member states of the Council of Europe at Rome in November 1950. Sponsored by the Council of Europe, this regional human rights charter went beyond the Universal Declaration of Human Rights of 1948 in (a) imposing *binding commitments* to provide in effect domestic remedies in regard to a number of the rights specified in the Universal Declaration; (b) the close and elaborate definition of such rights as it embraced, and of the exceptions and restrictions to each of such rights; (c) the establishment of a European Commission of Human Rights to investigate and report on violations of human rights at the instance of states parties, or—if the state against which complaint was laid, had so accepted—upon the petition of any person, non-governmental organization, or group of individuals within the jurisdiction of the state subject of the complaint. The Commission became competent to receive applications of the latter kind in July 1955, after, as required by the Convention, six states had accepted such right of individual recourse. Since July 1955, the number of accepting states has increased. The Convention also provided for a European Court of Human Rights with compulsory jurisdiction, to come into being upon at least eight states accepting such jurisdiction. This was achieved in September 1958, and the Court was set up in January 1959. It delivered its first judgment on 14 November 1960, in the Lawless Case. The Convention has since 1950 been amended and added to by a number of protocols.

This combination of an administrative and a curial jurisdiction, operating in an interrelated manner, has worked reasonably well, but it is far from providing direct access by an individual to the Court for any breach of a human right under the Convention. The European Commission of Human Rights indeed fulfils, in a certain measure, the function of screening complaints before the Court can take cognizance of them. The great majority of applications received by the Commission have in point of fact been declared inadmissible under the Convention because of failure to exhaust local remedies, lapse of a period of six months or more after final decision by a domestic court (article 26), activities of applicants aimed at the destruction of the rights and freedoms guaranteed by the Convention (article 17), and other grounds, such as the anonymity of the applicant. If the application is declared admissible by the Commission, the Commission's primary action, if it has been unable to dispose of the matter by conciliation, is to transmit its report on the question of a breach of a right under the Convention to the Committee of Ministers of the Council of Europe, which may decide upon the measures to be taken if there has been a breach, unless the matter is referred to the Court within a period of three months. As to the Court, only the states accepting its jurisdiction, and the Commission, but not individuals, have the right to bring a case before it.[33] A complainant has no direct right to be heard by the Court but, as decided in the Lawless Case, his point of view can be presented to the Court through delegates of the Commission, or in the Commission's report, or in his evidence, if he is called as a witness. The influence of the Court and its authority in the matter of European human rights are not to be minimized; both directly and indirectly, its decisions have led to changes in legislation or in administrative practices to conform with a state's obligations under the Convention, as for example in the Vagrancy Cases of 1971, which brought about amendments to Belgium's vagrancy legislation, and in the Golder Case of 1975 in which it held that a British prisoner, by reason of his right to a fair and public hearing of a civil claim for damages intended to be made by him (see article 6 of the Convention) could not be denied a right of access to legal advice by a solicitor, so that the prison rules prohibitive of such access called for amendment.[34] Even in the absence of a hearing by the Court, changes in national legislation have occurred, in particular, where it was sought to avoid an anticipated adverse decision.[35]

Another important instance of a regional human rights instrument is that of the Inter-American Convention on Human Rights, opened for signature on 22 November 1969. In addition to detailed definitions of human rights, provision is made for establishing an Inter-American Court of Human Rights; states parties wishing to accept the Court's

[33] On the procedure of the European Court of Human Rights, see H. Mosler, 'La procédure de la Cour Internationale de Justice et de la Cour Européenne des Droits de l'Homme' in *René Cassin: Amicorum Discipulorumque Liber* (Paris, 1969) I, pp. 196–212, and notes on the 'European Court of Human Rights: Organization and Operation', *New Law Journal* CXXII (1972), p. 247.

[34] See G. Triggs, 'Prisoners' Rights to Legal Advice and Access to the Courts: the Golder Decision by the European Court of Human Rights', *Australian Law Journal* L (1976), pp. 229–45.

[35] Cf. D. Schindler, 'Innerstaatliche Wirkungen der Entscheidungen der europäischen Menschenrechtorgane' in *Festschrift zum 70. Geburtstag von Dr Max Guldener* (Zürich, 1973), pp. 273–90.

jurisdiction may make declarations to this effect when ratifying or adhering to the Convention (see article 62). In this connection, reference may be made also to the important revision by the 1967 Protocol of Buenos Aires to the Charter of the Organization of American States (OAS), establishing the Inter-American Commission on Human Rights as a principal organ of the OAS, with the function of promoting respect for the human rights declared in the American Declaration of the Rights and Duties of Man of 1948, and with the additional mandate of keeping 'vigilance' over the observance of human rights pending the entry into force of the American Convention of Human Rights of 1969.[36]

This study of human rights and international law would be incomplete without some reference, however brief, to three points of some significance.

First, a number of important human rights are not rights of individuals, but collective rights, that is to say they are the rights of groups or peoples.[37] This is clear so far as concerns the right of self-determination, which broadly speaking is the right of a people to emancipation and to the control of its own government. Apart from the right of self-determination, there is the right of an ethnic group or of a people to physical existence as such, a right which is implicit in the provisions of the Genocide Convention of December 1948. Then also, there is the right of certain groups or minorities to maintain their own identity; such a right and the corresponding commitment of states are provided for in article 27 of the International Covenant on Civil and Political Rights in these terms: 'In those States in which ethnic, religious or linguistic minorities exist, persons belonging to such minorities shall not be denied the right, in community with other members of their group, to enjoy their own culture, to profess and practise their own religion, or to use their own language.'

Secondly, since 1967–8 a process has been set in motion of importing human rights rules and standards into that branch of international law traditionally known as the 'law of war' or the 'law of armed conflicts', being those recognized rules of international law prescribing the limits within which force may be used in respect to war and hostilities, and governing the humane treatment of individuals who may be involved, directly, in such struggles, as combatants or as non-combatants.[38] The main content of this branch of law was constituted by the four Geneva Conventions of 1949 on, respectively, the Amelioration of the Condition of the Wounded and Sick in Armed

[36] See T. Buergenthal, 'The Revised OAS Charter and the Protection of Human Rights', *American Journal of International Law* LXIX (1975), pp. 828–36.

[37] See Yoram Dinstein, 'Collective Human Rights of Peoples and Minorities', *International and Comparative Law Quarterly* XXV (1976), pp. 102–20.

[38] See R. R. Baxter, 'The Law of War' in Bos, *op. cit.*, pp. 107–24.

Forces in the Field, the Amelioration of the Condition of the Wounded, Sick and Shipwrecked Members of the Armed Forces at Sea, the Treatment of Prisoners of War, and the Protection of Civilian Persons in Time of War, and the regulations annexed to the Hague Convention Number IV of 1907 on the Laws and Customs of War on Land (more familiarly known as the 'Hague Rules' or the 'Hague Regulations'). One important step contributing to the present interrelation of human rights and the law of war was the resolution of the International Conference on Human Rights at Teheran in 1968, calling upon the Secretary-General of the United Nations to study the better application of human rights standards to the laws of war, and the necessity for additional conventions to supplement the above-mentioned Geneva Conventions of 1949. This was followed by the notable report of the Secretary-General, Document A/8052 of September 1970 bearing the title, 'Respect for Human Rights in Armed Conflicts', and by a number of resolutions of the General Assembly of the United Nations calling for the greater protection of human rights in armed conflicts.

As a result, there has been a fundamental change in terminology. The expression 'international humanitarian law applicable in armed conflicts' has now replaced the former traditional phrases, 'law of war' and 'law of armed conflicts'. The Geneva Conference which in the years 1974–7 held three sessions for the purpose of reaffirming the rules in the Geneva Conventions of 1949, and making the necessary revisions and updating of such rules or adding thereto in the light of post-1949 developments, bore the title of 'the Diplomatic Conference on the Reaffirmation and Development of International Humanitarian Law Applicable in Armed Conflicts'. Moreover, the international law institute which is foremost in the field in this branch of law is the International Institute of Humanitarian Law, at San Remo, Italy.

This important relationship between human rights and the rules of international law applicable in armed conflicts was well described by Professor Gerald Draper in these terms:

> Within the space of the last decade there has been an increasing awareness that where State revision of the Law of War had failed, State responsiveness to augmenting the regime of Human Rights could go some of the way to make good that defect. By a series of resolutions at Red Cross Conferences, by UN Conferences on Human Rights and by resolutions of the General Assembly *a bridge has been built between the Human Rights system and the Law of Armed Conflicts.* It seems to have been realized, not all at once, that what could not be achieved through a general revision of the Law of War might be partially secured by regarding the Law of War as something essentially complementary to the Human Rights regime [my italics].

According to Professor Draper, not only has the human rights system afforded 'a fundamental and novel approach' to the law of war and its revision, but it has led to 'awareness among the percipient that respect for human rights cannot be fragmented into time of peace and of war and that such rights are under maximum threat in time of war'.[39]

Indeed this 'bridge' created since 1967–8 between the law of human rights and the law of armed conflicts represents one of the most significant contributions of the human rights movement to the development of international law.

The third point of significance is that under the Helsinki Declaration adopted on 1 August 1975 by over thirty European states, together with Canada, the Holy See and the United States, at the Conference on Security and Cooperation in Europe, the participating states reaffirmed in Part VII of the Declaration pledges to observe human rights and fundamental freedoms, to respect the rights of minorities to equality before the law, and to endeavour jointly and separately, including in cooperation with the United Nations, to promote universal and effective respect for such rights and freedoms. The Helsinki Declaration was particularly invoked by President Carter of the United States in 1977–8 in his moves for the wider observance of human rights throughout the world. Even if the Helsinki Declaration is like the Universal Declaration not to be deemed a binding international treaty, these statements, subscribed to by so many important states, represent an acknowledgment that the subject of human rights is not one within the sphere of a state's reserved jurisdiction but is of international concern.

[39] Draper, *op. cit.*, at pp. 337 and 339.

Suggested reading

I

Any standard edition of the following:

Thomas Hobbes, *Leviathan*, especially chapters 13–30.
John Locke, *Second Treatise of Civil Government*.
J. J. Rousseau, *The Social Contract* and *Discourse on the Origin of Inequality*.
Edmund Burke, *Reflections on the Revolution in France*.
Thomas Paine, *The Rights of Man*.
Jeremy Bentham, *Introduction to the Principles of Morals and Legislation*, especially chapters 1–2.

II

David Hume, *Theory of Politics*, edited by Frederick Watkins (London, Nelson, 1951).
D. G. Ritchie, *Natural Rights* (London, Allen and Unwin, 1894). Several times reprinted, this volume contains the texts of the Virginian Declaration of Rights, 1776, the French Declarations of Rights of 1789, 1793 and 1795, and the preamble to the French Constitution of 1848 as well as an extract from the American Declaration of Independence.
Jacques Maritain, *The Rights of Man and Natural Law* (New York, Charles Scribner's, 1943).
Margaret Macdonald, 'Natural Rights' in *Proceedings of the Aristotelian Society* n.s. XLVII (1946–47), reprinted in P. Laslett, editor, *Philosophy, Politics and Society*, first series (Oxford, Blackwell, 1956), pp. 35–55 and in A. I. Melden (see below), pp. 40–60.
UNESCO, *Human Rights*, a symposium edited by J. Maritain (New York, Columbia University Press, 1949).
H. L. A. Hart, 'Are there any Natural Rights?' in *Philosophical Review* LXIV (1955), pp. 175–91, reprinted in A. Quinton (see below), pp. 53–66 and in Melden, pp. 61–75.

D. D. Raphael, editor, *Political Theory and the Rights of Man* (London, Macmillan, 1967).

A. Quinton, editor, *Political Philosophy* (London , Oxford University Press, 1967).

Howard E. Kiefer and Milton K. Munitz, editors, *Ethics and Social Justice* (Albany, State University of New York Press, 1968), especially pp. 252–332.

A. I. Melden, editor, *Human Rights* (Belmont, California, Wadsworth Publishing Co., 1970). This contains, apart from the reprints of Macdonald and Hart, selections from Locke and Bentham, articles by G. Vlastos, R. Wasserstrom and H. Morris, and the texts of the Virginian Declaration of Rights, the Declaration of The Rights of Man and of Citizens of 1789 and the United Nations Universal Declaration of Human Rights of 1948, together with an extract from the American Declaration of Independence.

Maurice Cranston, *What are Human Rights?* (London, Bodley Head, 1973). This contains the texts of the Universal Declaration of Human Rights, 1948, the International Covenant on Economic, Social and Cultural Rights, 1966, the International Covenant on Civil and Political Rights, 1966, and the European Convention for the Protection of Human Rights and Fundamental Freedoms, 1966.

Contributors

Christopher Arnold is Senior Lecturer in Law at the University of Sydney. He was born in London in 1943 and educated at University College, London, where he read law, and at Bedford College, London and Balliol College, Oxford, where he read philosophy. He is a barrister-at-law of Gray's Inn and has practised law in the City of London. He was Lecturer in Law at University College, London, before going to Sydney University. He has published a number of articles in law journals on jurisprudence and philosophy of law.

Stanley I. Benn is Professorial Fellow in Philosophy in the Institute of Advanced Studies of the Australian National University and a Fellow of the Academy of the Social Sciences in Australia. Born in West Ham, England, in 1920, he was educated at the West Ham Secondary School and at the London School of Economics, graduating in economics and government. He was Lecturer in Government in the University College (later the University) of Southampton from 1948 until his move to the Australian National University in 1962. He is co-author, with R. S. Peters, of *Social Principles and the Democratic State* (1959), and co-editor, with G. W. Mortimore, of *Rationality and the Social Sciences* (1976), to which he also contributed. He is the author of thirteen articles on topics in political philosophy in the *Encyclopedia of Philosophy* (1967). His other contributions to volumes of essays and periodicals have been concerned mainly with the explication and elaboration of basic principles and ideals in moral and political theory, most recently in connection with a study of freedom and autonomy.

Nathan Glazer, Professor of Education and Social Structure in the Graduate School of Education of Harvard University since 1969, was born in New York City in 1923 and educated at the (then) City College of New York, the University of Pennsylvania and Harvard University.

He has been a member of the editorial staff of *Commentary* magazine and of Doubleday-Anchor books and, from 1953–1959, Professor of Sociology in the University of California at Berkeley. He is co-editor of *The Public Interest* magazine and the author of numerous books on sociological and ethnic problems, including *The Lonely Crowd* and *Faces in the Crowd* (both with David Riesman, 1950 and 1952), *American Judaism* (1957), *The Social Basis of American Communism* (1961), *Beyond the Melting Pot* (with D. Moynihan, 1963), *Remembering the Answers* (1970) and, most recently, *Affirmative Discrimination* (1976). He has spent a year visiting and studying in Japan and has worked as an urban sociologist in Washington; in 1977 he visited Australia and took part in the World Congress on Philosophy of Law and Social Philosophy there on a distinguished visitor's award of the Australian-American Educational Foundation.

Eugene Kamenka is Foundation Professor of the History of Ideas in the Institute of Advanced Studies of the Australian National University and has been (in 1973, 1974 and 1976) Visiting Professor in the Faculty of Law in the University of Sydney. He is a Fellow of the Academy of the Social Sciences in Australia and Fellow and secretary of the Australian Academy of the Humanities. Born in Cologne, Germany, in 1928, of Russian Jewish parents, Professor Kamenka was educated in Australia in the Sydney Technical High School, the University of Sydney and the Australian National University. He has worked and taught in Israel, England, Germany, the United States, Canada, the USSR and Singapore. His books include *The Ethical Foundations of Marxism* (1962), *Marxism and Ethics* (1969) and *The Philosophy of Ludwig Feuerbach* (1970); he has edited *A World in Revolution?* (1970), *Paradigm for Revolution? The Paris Commune 1871–1971* (1972), *Nationalism—The Nature and Evolution of an Idea* (1973), with R. S. Neale *Feudalism, Capitalism and Beyond* (1975) and, with Robert Brown and A. E. S. Tay, *Law and Society: The Crisis in Legal Ideals* (1978). He is general editor of this series, 'Ideas and Ideologies'.

John Kleinig is Senior Lecturer in Philosophy in Macquarie University, Sydney. Born in 1942, he was educated at Hale School, the University of Western Australia and the Australian National University, where he completed a doctorate in 1968. He has been a visiting part-time lecturer in the University of Sydney in the fields of jurisprudence, philosophy of education and philosophical theology. During 1975, he spent periods as Visiting Scholar in the University of London Institute of Education and as Visiting Associate Professor in Philosophy at the Rockefeller University, New York. He is the author of *Punishment and Desert* (1973) and articles in ethics, social philosophy, philosophy of education, and philosophical theology. He is the editor of *Interchange*.

Kenneth R. Minogue is Reader in Political Science in the London School of Economics, a member of the editorial board of the *British Journal of Political Science* and of the Social Science Research Council of the United Kingdom. Born in Palmerston North, New Zealand, in 1930, he was educated at Sydney Boys' High School, the University of Sydney and the London School of Economics, where he has taught political science since 1956. He is the author of *The Liberal Mind* (1962), *Nationalism* (1967) and *The Concept of a University* (1973) and of articles on political theory and the history of ideas in academic journals and journals of opinion, and joint editor, with A. R. de Crespigny, of *Contemporary Political Philosophers* (1975). He has been a visiting fellow in the History of Ideas Unit in the Australian National University and has recently been asked to draft a comprehensive educational 'master-plan' for the Pahlavi University of Shiraz in Iran. He is now working on a history of the idea of the social contract and on a study of the logical and rhetorical structure of ideology.

Joseph Gabriel Starke, barrister-at-law, is a Queen's Counsel in Australia for the State of New South Wales and the Australian Capital Territory (Canberra), and is also Professor of Humanitarian Law in the International Institute of Humanitarian Law, San Remo, Italy. He is editor of *The Australian Law Journal*, editor of *The Australian Digest of International Law*, and a member of the panel of international arbitrators, International Court of Justice, The Hague. Born in Perth, Western Australia, in 1911, he was educated at Perth Modern School and the University of Western Australia, gaining a Rhodes Scholarship, and subsequently at Oxford University, where he was awarded the Vinerian Law Scholarship for 1934. In 1934–5 he studied at the University of Geneva and the Geneva Post-Graduate Institute of International Studies, where he was a pupil of Hans Kelsen. He was a member of the League of Nations Secretariat, Geneva, 1935–40, and served as deputy secretary of the League's Status of Women Commission. His published books and articles range over a number of areas of the law, especially international law, the law of contracts, town planning law, law of human rights, and forensic psychology. He is the author of *An Introduction to International Law* (8th edn, 1977), *Studies in International Law* (1965), *The ANZUS Treaty Alliance* (1966), *The Law of Town and Country Planning in New South Wales* (1966), *An Introduction to the Science of Peace* (1968), and *The Validity of Psycho-Analysis* (1973), and co-author, with P. F. P. Higgins, of the third Australian edition (1974) of *Cheshire & Fifoot on Contracts*. He was

Visiting Professor at the University of Paris in 1967 and at the Max Planck Institute, Heidelberg, in 1972.

Alice Erh-Soon Tay is Professor of Jurisprudence in the University of Sydney and a member of the Australian National Commission for UNESCO and its specialist Committee for the Social Sciences. She was born in Singapore in 1934 and educated at Raffles Girls' School, Singapore, Lincoln's Inn and the Australian National University, where she took her doctorate with a thesis on 'The Concept of Possession in the Common Law'. She has practised in criminal law and lectured in law in the (then) University of Malaya in Singapore and the Australian National University, spent 1965–6 and parts of 1973 and 1977–8 as a visiting research worker and professor in the Faculty of Law in Moscow State University and the Institute of State and Law of the Academy of Sciences of the USSR, and been senior fellow at the Russian Institute and the Research Institute on Communist Affairs of Columbia University, New York, and in the East-West Center of the University of Hawaii. She is the author of numerous articles on common law, jurisprudence, comparative law, Soviet law and Chinese law, and of several contributions to the *Encyclopedia of Soviet Law*, besides being co-author, with her husband, Eugene Kamenka, of a forthcoming book, *Marxism and the Theory of Law*. She is an executive member of the International Association for Philosophy of Law and Social Philosophy and served as president of the Association's Extraordinary World Congress, held in Sydney and Canberra in 1977.

Carl Wellman is Professor of Philosophy in Washington University in Saint Louis, a member of the executive committee of the Western Division of the American Philosophical Association, and the secretary general of the International Association for Philosophy of Law and Social Philosophy. Born in 1926, he attended the University of Arizona, where he graduated with highest distinction and a Phi Beta Kappa key in 1949. He received his master's degree from Harvard University in 1951 and his doctorate from the same institution in 1954. He also studied for one year at the University of Cambridge on a Sheldon Travelling Fellowship. He has received an American Council of Learned Societies fellowship (1965–6), the Uhrig Award for Outstanding Teaching (1968), and a National Endowment for the Humanities senior fellowship (1972–3). In addition to various philosophical papers, he has written *The Language of Ethics* (1961), *Challenge and Response* (1971), and *Morals and Ethics* (1975).

Index